Seasons of Time

by Diane E. DiSanto

Acknowledgments

The author has unending gratitude to Judith E. Fedo, her friend and editor, who lovingly edited text and content with patience and artistic acuity, helping to shape its outcome.

I am very grateful to VA Graphics and its entire design staff for their encouragement and ideas which helped make my dream into a reality.

Thanks to Scott Roberts for the illustration of my grandmother's watch shown throughout the book.

I am greatly indebted to my friends at Scrap Mania who believed my heritage designs needed to be shared with others.

I give more thanks than I can ever express to my husband, Bill DiSanto, for his steadfast faith in me and this book. Without his love and support, I would not have been able to pursue this venture.

Finally, I thank God for His gifts of inspiration and creativity as well as His servant, Pastor Mac Hammond, of Living Word Christian Center in Brooklyn Park, Minnesota. Pastor Mac used "Breakthrough to Destiny" to teach me about God's plan for my life and to follow my passion.

"Eye has not seen, nor ear heard, nor have entered into the heart of man the things which God has prepared for those who love Him."
— 1 Corinthians 2:9

To everything there is a *Season* and a *Time* to every purpose under heaven.

Ecclesiastes 3:1

Diane's Ideas for Heritage Design

❧ Scan photos and items that may not be acid-free and print on acid-free paper or photo paper. Original photos are quite vulnerable to fluctuating humidity. Keep originals safely stored at a constant temperature between 65 and 75 degrees otherwise chemical changes occur that cause deterioration.

- Scan 3-dimensional objects too thick to use in an album format.

- Color coordinate the tones from your heritage images, with a variety of paper and objects to unify your designs.

- Avoid using more than 3 colors per layout, but include variations of those hues.

- Use dye pads to "age" paper and photos when trying to match colors in a layout.

- Choose colors from the background paper for matting.

- Generally, bright primary colors and pure whites do not belong in a heritage album dated before the 1950's.

- Select special papers to create a specific mood:

  - Muted lacey paper with feminine photos

  - Tailored and geometric paper with masculine photos

  - Rustic paper with farming or woodsy photos

- Search for fonts appropriate to the mood and era of the layout.

- Use contrasting textures to create energy.

- Avoid using cartoons and overused images.

- Layer and tear papers to create interesting borders. Repeat these techniques to develop a sense of transition and unity from one page to another.

- Use poems, quotations or Scripture to augment your journaling.

- Avoid isolating objects, photos, and text boxes except to show emphasis. When the objects overlap, they relate to each other.

- Play with color related pattern-on-pattern for exciting variety.

- When you don't have a journal from which to work, see it as a precious opportunity to interview family. Record the interviews when possible and use photos and memorabilia to spark memories.

Scan and experiment with ephemera and memorabilia:

Postcards	Memorial cards	Fabric pieces
Certificates	Brochures	Hair/hair ribbons
Diplomas	Receipts	Wallpaper samples
Newspaper articles	Clothing	Crocheted handkerchiefs
Prayer cards	Stamps	Coupons
Doilies	Invitations	Report cards
Dried flowers	Letters/envelopes	Shoes
Family jewelry	Licenses	Greeting cards
Fair ribbons	Awards	Bonds
Ticket stubs	Money/coins	Toys

Dedication

This book is dedicated to my daughter, Stacey McCloskey, who through her death, taught me to appreciate life and to my son, John DiSanto, whose strength to overcome difficulties gives me hope; to my sisters, Carlene Hoeschen and Janice Brunk; and my dad, Thorwald Johannsen for always appreciating and encouraging my passion for creativity; to my best friend, Pat DeLaMater, who shows me how to live each day to its fullest and to my mother, Leona Johannsen, who taught me at a very young age, the *joy* of scrapbooking.

Author's Biography

Diane E. DiSanto has been a scrapbooker for more than 50 years and has taught scrapbook classes for 8 years. She is skilled in computer photo restoration and editing. The author is currently accepting commissions to design and create scrapbooks relating to any theme or topic.

Diane has worked for Medtronic, Inc. over 25 years as a layout designer in medical devices. The author is also an accredited interior designer whose interests include reading, writing poetry, and landscaping. She lives in Ramsey, Minnesota with her husband, Bill DiSanto.

Photo by Judith E. Fedo

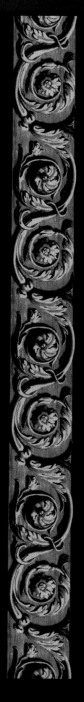

This album is a tribute to the early years of my parents, Leona Emma Beermann Johannsen and Thorwald William Louis Johannsen. Most of the stories and information have come from the journals of my mother, Leona, and are recorded here just as she penned them.

Great honor, respect and love is given to you, my parents.

Diane E. DiSanto

The most treasured heirlooms are the sweet memories of our family. — *Unknown*

Every book deserves a preface or explanation of its purpose. The preface might include a warm or poignant story to indicate the content of the album. My heritage album is meant to reveal in an artistic way, the story of my mother Leona Johannsen's life as recorded in her journals. Mother's writings reflect many passages of life — her **Seasons of Time**.

Supplies List

Paper and Stickers: Frances Meyer
Cardstock: Bazzill Basics Paper
Computer font: Montague (Internet)

Remember me

Frieda Caroline Reinhardt was born
July 23, 1878 in Neinburg, Germany.
She died May 25, 1971 at the age of 93.

Louie Tinnemann was born on
November 22, 1876 in Neinburg,
Germany. He was a glass blower
and died of cancer at the age of 27 on
October 28, 1903.

Using collage-design scrapbook paper reduces design time and also offers
inspiration for color choices. A border punch was used on this page to soften an
otherwise angular photo frame.

God does not stifle our tears; He turns them into joy. — Janette Oke

Treasure each other in the recognition that we do not know how long we shall have each other.

— Joshua Loth Liebman

Louie Tinnemann married Frieda Caroline Reinhardt in Neinburg, Germany on September 5, 1896.
He and Freida had two children, Karolina (Lena) Friederike Louisa and her brother, William.
In 1907, Frieda and her two children sailed to America . This picture is of Neinburg a/Weser.

The punch was used again to enhance the frame surrounding the landscape photo, which also created harmony between these pages.

Setting down roots in a new place can seem to threaten our survival. But given enough time, it usually allows us more room to expand.
— *Vivian Elisabeth Glyck*

By faith he sojourned in the land of promise as in a foreign country . . .
— *Hebrews 11:9*

Supplies List

Paper:	Paper Pizazz by Hot Off The Press; Rocky Mountain Scrapbook Company; K & Company
Stickers:	Colorbök
Edge punch:	Fiskars Brands, Inc.
Corner rounder punch:	Marvy Uchida
Computer Font:	Diploma, The Print Shop/Broderbund

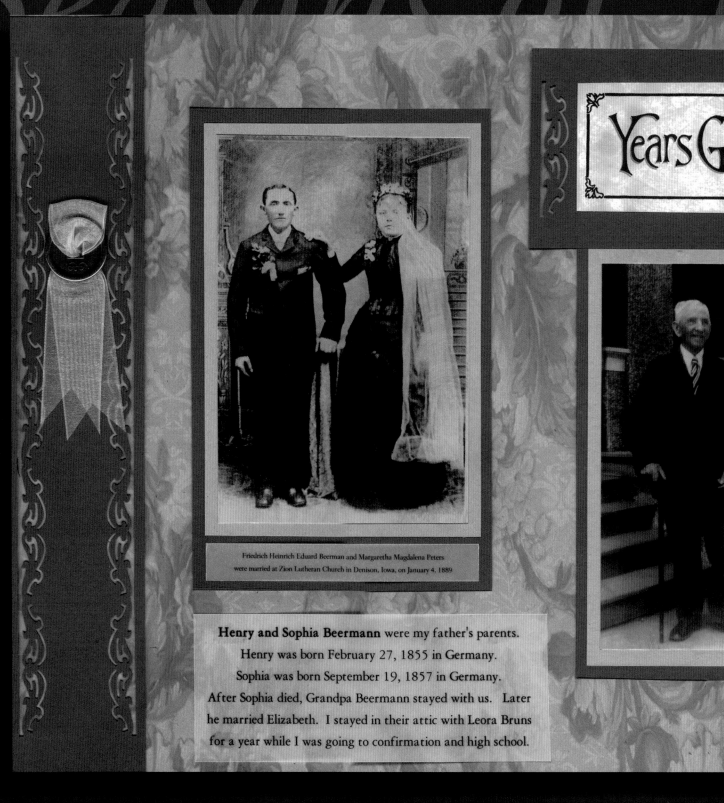

Years G

Friedrich Heinrich Eduard Beerman and Margaretha Magdalena Peters
were married at Zion Lutheran Church in Denison, Iowa, on January 4, 1889

Henry and Sophia Beermann were my father's parents.
Henry was born February 27, 1855 in Germany.
Sophia was born September 19, 1857 in Germany.
After Sophia died, Grandpa Beermann stayed with us. Later
he married Elizabeth. I stayed in their attic with Leora Bruns
for a year while I was going to confirmation and high school.

The purchased page topper "Years Gone By" and the vellum used for journaling
were originally white. By using a stamping dye pad an antique look was achieved.

The technique for this is to rub a make-up sponge across the dye pad then
gently blot the surface you wish to antique. Be sure to allow the dye to dry
thoroughly before assembling the page.

Most assuredly, I say to you, he who hears my word and believes in Him who sent Me has everlasting life,
and shall not come into judgment, but has passed from death into life. — John 5:24

Carl H. Beermann and his first wife, Alma
Loewe, who died one year later in childbirth.

Through my grandmother's eyes,
I can see more clearly the way things used to be,
the way things ought to be, and most important of all,
the way things really are.

— *Ed Cunningham*

Love is everything. Love is the passion of the soul.
It is the very strength upon which we live and breathe,
hope and dream. — Unknown

Supplies List

Paper:	The Family Archives LLC
Cardstock:	Paper Garden
Vellum:	Paper Garden
Page topper:	Deja Views® by The C-Thru® Ruler Company
Edge Punch:	Fiskars Brands, Inc.
Dye Pad:	Memories/Sand, Stewart Superior Corporation
Other:	Coins, ribbon
Computer font:	Amery, The Print Shop/Broderbund

Bridesmaids

Lena Tinnemann, as a bridesmaid, at
Aunt Francis and Uncle Louise's Wedding in 1913

One of the keys to good design is to embellish an image so the viewer's eye is drawn to it. On this page, there is light value lettering and a light, lacey textured handmade paper used to emphasize the photo. Experiment with a variety of cardstock colors under patterned vellum to achieve an appropriate mood for the photo and journaling.

A heart full of love can reach beyond all fear. — Unknown

Lena Tinnemann born October 26, 1897 at Neinburg a/weser in Germany. Her family name was Karolina Friedericka Louisa Tinnemann. Her parents were Frieda Reinhardt Tinnemann and Louie Tinnemann. She grew up in Germany until she was 9 years old. She then came to the U.S.A. with her mother and brother, Bill, on a ship. Her mother, Frieda, married again to William Hoffmeier and settled at his place near Buck Grove, Iowa. Buck Grove was a small town. My mother didn't get along with her step father, so she left home when she was a teen-ager. She worked at motels until she married Carl Henry George Beermann.

A sense of depth is implied by having the floral sticker overlap the journal box and the lacey background paper. This technique also unifies the materials.

Blessed are those who dwell in Your house;
They will still be praising You.
Blessed is the man whose strength is in You,
Whose heart is set on pilgrimage.
— Psalm 84:4, 5

Supplies List

Paper:	Anna Griffin
Vellum:	Autumn Leaves
Cardstock:	Bazzill Basics Paper
Handmade paper:	Creative Imaginations
Stickers:	K & Company
Photo corners:	Frances Meyer
Paper topper/title:	Little Extras
Computer font:	Cotillion, The Print Shop/Broderbund

Father

Mehrere Trauungen in verflossener Woche.

Eine Anzahl populäre Liebespaare schlossen den Bund auf Lebensdauer.

Im lutherischen Pfarrhause traute Pastor Frese am Mittwochvormittag Herrn Carl Beermann und Frl. Lina Tinnemann, beide aus der Buck Grove Umgegend, vor den Zeugen Herr und Frau Emil Bruns, Otto Beermann und Frl. Ida Wiese. Der Bräutigem ist ein Sohn unseres Freundes Henry Beermann, ein junger Mann von bestem Charakter, und die Braut ist eine Tochter von Frau Wilhelm Hoffmeier, ebenfalls eine geachtete und beliebte junge Dame. Möge dem jungen Ehepaare ein glücklicher Ehestand beschieden sein.

Carl H. Beermann born July 21, 1884 near Denison, Iowa. He grew up on a farm between Buck Grove and Denison, Iowa. His parents were Henry Beermann born February 27, 1855 and Sophia Rodermund Beermann born September 19, 1857, both born in Germany.

Newsprint is used throughout this album, but never in its original form.
All newsprint has been scanned and printed on acid free paper.

If there is a reason to include the original newsprint, consider using products available in most scrapbook stores that will seal the acid elements which would otherwise leach into the photos and cause irreparable damage.

This day I will marry my friend; The one I laugh with, live for, dream with, love. — Unknown

Lena Tinnemann and Carl H. Beermann
Lena born October 26, 1897   Carl born July 21, 1884
Married December 22, 1915
Died March 13, 1976   Died October 23, 1951

A scrapbook kit was used to coordinate
these pages and a decorative corner punch
duplicated the sticker designs that were
applied to the cream colored photo mat.

Supplies List

Scrapbook kit:	Time and Again, Deja Views® by The C-Thru® Ruler Company
Corner punch:	Anna Griffin
Corner rounder punch:	Marvy Uchida
Computer font:	Buckingham, The Print Shop/Broderbund

The birthday of my life has come,
my love is come to me.
— Christina Georgina Rossetti

And now abide faith, hope, love, these three;
but the greatest of these is love.
— Corinthians 13:13

Wedding Party of My Parents

Their wedding attendants were Anna Sophie Mina Beermann and her husband, Emil F. Bruns, Otto Herman Beermann and Ida Dieber.

The designer papers and stickers used here created continuity between these pages. Coordinated materials are great to use when you wish to complete pages quickly.

Most scrapbookers use plain cardstock, vellum, and paper for titles and journaling backgrounds. For variety, the text was printed on a patterned background paper and accented with solid color matting. Experiment with your materials.

Love does not consist in gazing at each other, but in looking outward together in the same direction.

— Antoine De Saint - Exupery

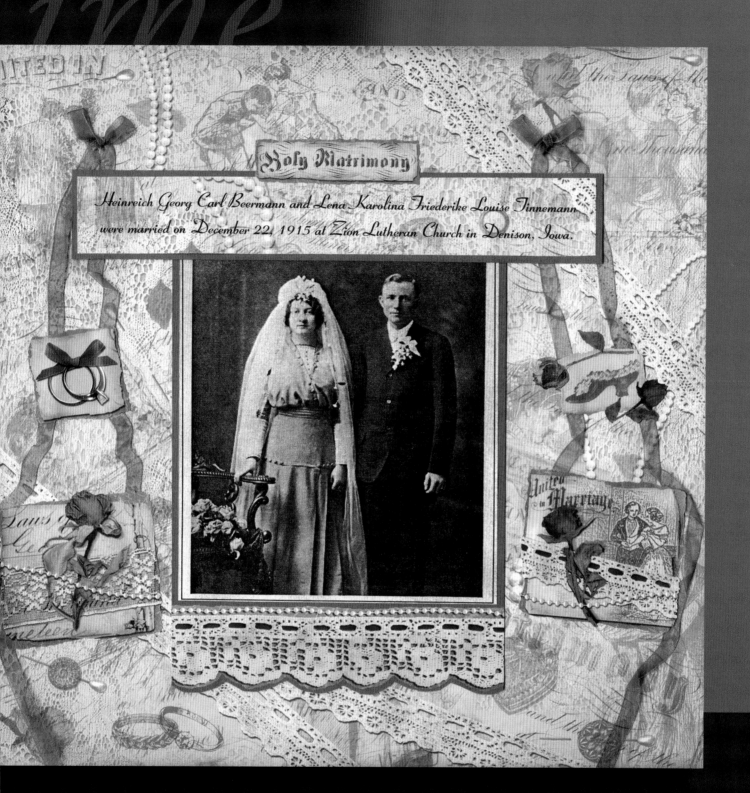

Holy Matrimony

Heinreich Georg Carl Beermann and Lena Karolina Friederike Louise Tinnemann were married on December 22, 1915 at Zion Lutheran Church in Denison, Iowa.

But whoever keeps his word, truly the love of God is perfected in him. By this we know that we are in Him. — 1 John 2:5

Grow old along with me the best is yet to be, the last of life for which the first was made.
— Robert Browning

What lies behind us and what lies before us are tiny matters compared to what lies within us.
— Unknown

Supplies List

Paper and Stickers: Karen Foster Design
Cardstock: Bazzill Basics Paper
Button: Dress It Up, Jesse James and Co.
Beaded fringe: 'Tis the Season distributed by Jo-Ann Stores, Inc.
Eyelet: Making Memories
Dye pad: Memories/Sand, Stewart Superior Corporation
Other: Ribbon
Computer font: Fairy Scroll Display (Internet)
Cornet, The Print Shop/Broderbund

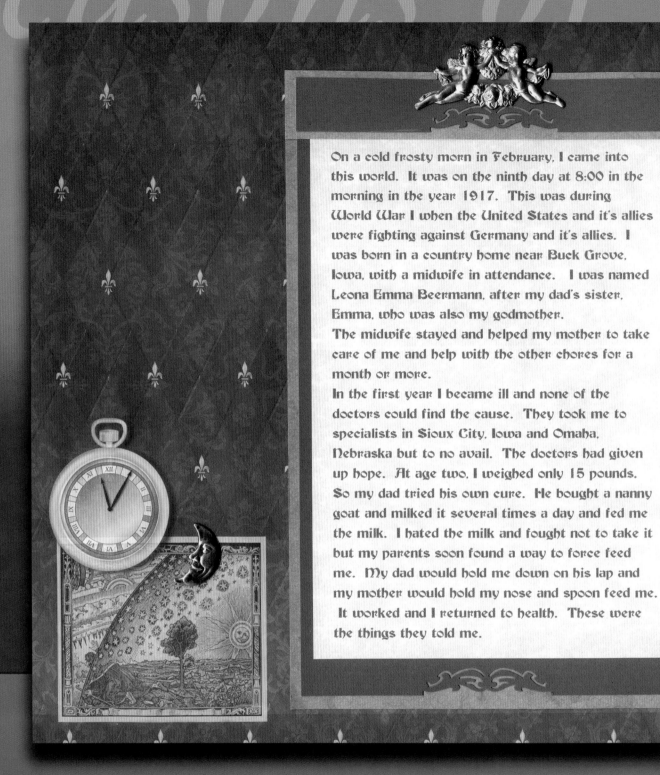

On a cold frosty morn in February, I came into this world. It was on the ninth day at 8:00 in the morning in the year 1917. This was during World War I when the United States and it's allies were fighting against Germany and it's allies. I was born in a country home near Buck Grove, Iowa, with a midwife in attendance. I was named Leona Emma Beermann, after my dad's sister, Emma, who was also my godmother.

The midwife stayed and helped my mother to take care of me and help with the other chores for a month or more.

In the first year I became ill and none of the doctors could find the cause. They took me to specialists in Sioux City, Iowa and Omaha, Nebraska but to no avail. The doctors had given up hope. At age two, I weighed only 15 pounds. So my dad tried his own cure. He bought a nanny goat and milked it several times a day and fed me the milk. I hated the milk and fought not to take it but my parents soon found a way to force feed me. My dad would hold me down on his lap and my mother would hold my nose and spoon feed me. It worked and I returned to health. These were the things they told me.

How fortunate are we whose family events have been recorded. My sisters and I never knew about our mother's sickly childhood until we read her journals after her death. The few moments it takes to record life's events conveys precious information to future generations.

START JOURNALING!

The rustle of an angel's wing is silenced by our dreams. — Diane E. DiSanto

I have heard your prayer, I have seen your tears; surely I will heal you. — 2 Kings 20:5

Born to Carl and Lena Beermann

Leona Emma Beermann

Experiment with contrasting elements to create an unexpected mood. The elegant fleur-de-lis background on these pages contrasts with the sweet simplicity of the baby photo and the story of Mother's first years. The golden charms add a sense of whimsy to this refined layout.

The soul is healed by being with children. — Dostoevsky

Behold, children are a heritage from the Lord . . . — Psalm 127:3

Supplies List

Paper: Paper Pizazz by Hot Off The Press; K & Company
Cardstock: Paper Garden
Edge Punch: Fiskars Brands, Inc.
Charms: Source unknown
Computer font: Buckingham, The Print Shop/Broderbund

Frieda would sleep in the crib in our parents' room, but my brother and I had to sleep in a cold upstairs room on a feather tick. Each morning we would run down and dress behind the hot stove, long underwear and all. We did this fast, also threw on a coat, scarf and overshoes if necessary to go to the "JOHN". It was a little "two holer" built outside, also known as the "back house". We didn't waste any time out there, especially when it got below zero.

We lived in this old, old house on a 160 acre farm. We had no conveniences. We had to pump all our water and carry it to the house. We used a water pail and dipper for drinking and a 5 gallon pail which we called a slop pail to carry out all waste water. Our baths were taken in a washtub behind a pot-bellied stove, which dad had stoked up before we got up in the morning. I was the oldest child, my brother, Vernon, was born two and a half years after me on August 9, 1919. My sister, Frieda, was born October 27, 1922.

In the kitchen, besides the water pail, washbasin, cupboard, table and chairs, we had an old black range (cook stove) with a warming oven and reservoir. The reservoir kept the water in it warm, while the stove was burning cobs and wood. Mostly cobs, that Vern and I picked up by the bushel basket after the pigs had eaten the corn off of them. On Saturdays we could spend the day, filling a big wagon, dad had placed in the hog yard, with cobs to burn in the stove. I also remember drying our shoes and mittens and warming our feet in the oven.

I could almost hear children's voices as I read Mother's evocative journaling. The poor quality of these photos doesn't seem to be an issue when surrounded by the re-telling of mom's early childhood days. Note how using the same background paper creates harmony between these pages.

Family ties are growing bonds nourished by love and laughter, and a thousand everyday events that are cherished ever after. — *Unknown*

We are hemmed round with mystery, and the greatest mysteries are contained in what we see and do every day. — *Henri Frederic Amiel*

Early Childhood Days

THE HOMESTEAD

On laundry day, we'd carry the water for a big copper boiler that was heated on the stove and then carried to the washer that was powered by hand, by pushing a stick handle back and forth. We filled two tubs with water for rinsing and then mom hung it all out on the clothesline summer and winter. Sometimes the long johns would come in so stiff with ice, they could "stand alone".

On Saturday my mom would bake lots of fresh bread and rolls, and it was our job to churn the butter in a barrel churn. Sometimes it took forever and we both got tired of churning. I remember once someone did not have the lid fastened and all the cream went on the floor and on my brother. There was some screaming then.

The stickers on this page help to capture and enhance the images of her story. The use of tan photo corners helped set apart the journaling from the background paper without using a full mat. Variety in technique helps keep pages fresh and interesting.

Supplies List

Paper: Colorbök; Daisy D's Paper Company; Memories Forever/Westrim Crafts
Stickers: Tumblebeasts Stickers
Punch-out: Fiskars Brands, Inc.
Photo corners: Canson, Inc.
Corner punch: Marvy Uchida
Lettering: QuicKutz
Computer font: Missy BT (Internet)

I am the bread of life. — John 6:48

The wonder of life we experience as a child gives hope to a lifetime of adventure. — Unknown

History

*W*hen we were very small we played together under the summer trees, picked dandelions to carry home, drew in the dust of shadowed lanes, stamped in mud, kicked joyfully through Autumn leaves.

Age was no concern of ours. The seasons gave their gifts and gave no hint that time would mark us.

But the trees are felled, the meadows vanished, the lanes forgotten.

And we are growing old, my friend. Walk with me, then, and talk of those lost times — still vivid in our minds. Still living in our hearts.

Life is still good — but we live in both worlds.

We recognize the children that we were shining in one another's eyes.

And smile — knowing that nothing good is ever lost.

PAM BROWN, b. 1928

Nature Walk

Texture stimulates our senses. These two pages were meant to be a playground for our senses and draw out the child in us. The fragile butterfly wings, a brittle autumn leaf, the rough grid of window screen, the softness of Mother's hair, and the curving paths of stitchery, join forces to create two lively pages.

Search for poems that emotionally tie in to your theme. Poetry can change a merely attractive page into a poignant experience.

Beauty in things exists in the mind which contemplates them. — David Hume

Treasures from the Past

I always wore a bow in my hair,

from my grandmother Hoffmeier,

until I had my hair cut into a bob.

Legacy

Supplies List

Paper:	Rebecca Sower Designs (EK Success)	*Dye pad:*	Memories/Sand, Stewart Superior Corporation
Vellum:	Paper Garden	*Tag in a bag:*	DMD, Inc.
Mesh/Maruyama:	Magenta	*Other:*	Mom's hair, grandma's thread and
Cardstock:	Bazzill Basic Paper		floral pictures, sources unknown
Stickers:	Karen Foster Design; me & my BIG ideas	*Butterflies:*	The Print Shop/Broderbund
Cutouts:	Fresh Cuts ™ Printed Accents by	*Computer font:*	Edwardian Script ITC (Internet)
	Rebecca Sower Designs (EK Success)		
Punch-outs:	Fiskars Brands, Inc.		

IN SEPTEMBER 1922, I STARTED TO SCHOOL. IT WAS A ONE ROOM SCHOOL ON THE EDGE OF TOWN. IT WAS HARDER FOR ME THAN MOST KIDS AS I HAD TO LEARN A NEW LANGUAGE. MY FOLKS TAUGHT US GERMAN AND THAT'S WHAT WE ALL SPOKE UNTIL I LEARNED THE AMERICAN LANGUAGE AT SCHOOL. LOTS OF MISUNDERSTANDING. THE TEACHER ASKED US TO BRING GOODS (MATERIAL) FOR AN ART PROJECT AND I BROUGHT WOOD. MOST EMBARRASSING. IT DOESN'T TAKE LONG FOR YOUNGSTERS TO CATCH ON. MY BROTHER LEARNED FROM ME AND DIDN'T HAVE MY PROBLEMS. OUR SCHOOL CONSISTED OF ROWS OF DESKS BUILT FOR TWO. IF TEACHER HAD A BEHAVIOR PROBLEM, SHE WOULD MAKE US SET WITH A BOY. VERY HUMILIATING. UP FRONT, IN FRONT OF TEACHERS DESK, WAS A LONG RECITATION BENCH. WHEN SHE WOULD CALL OUR GRADE NUMBER WE WOULD GO SIT ON THE BENCH AND ANSWER HER QUESTIONS (HOPEFULLY). THEN WE WOULD GO BACK TO OUR DESK AND THE NEXT CLASS WOULD GO UP (AS MANY AS 8 OR 10). HAD A WATER FOUNTAIN AT SCHOOL AND ONE COMMUNITY CUP. TWO BY TWO WE WOULD GO TO FETCH WATER FROM SOMEONE'S HOUSE AND USUALLY PLAY ON THE WAY. A COALHOUSE WAS BUILT ON THE BACK OF THE SCHOOL. TEACHER WOULD STOKE THE FIRE EACH MORNING IN THIS POTBELLIED STOVE THAT HAD A HUGE JACKET AROUND IT. I REMEMBER FREEZING MANY TIMES. ALSO REMEMBER MICE IN THE COALHOUSE. SOME TIMES THEY'D BE IN TEACHERS DESK DRAWER. NOT SURE IF THE BOYS PUT IT THERE OR IF THEY FOUND THEIR OWN WAY. WE ALWAYS BROUGHT COLD LUNCHES IN A SYRUP PAIL - 1/2 GALLON AND SOME HAD GALLON ONES. AND I THINK WE ALL DRANK OUT OF THE SAME CUP. WE STARTED OUR DAY WITH THE PLEDGE OF ALLEGIANCE TO THE FLAG AND SOMETIMES WE WOULD SING SONGS AND GET TO CHOOSE THE SONGS. I USUALLY CHOSE A PEPPY ONE, "DIXIE LAND." IN THE AFTERNOON, SHE WOULD PLAY THE VICTROLA AND WE WOULD MARCH AROUND THE ROOM OR DO EXERCISE TO MUSIC AFTER SCHOOL WE WALKED HOME (NO BUSSES). I HAD A FRIEND LESTER. HIS DAD RAN THE HARDWARE STORE IN BUCK GROVE. LESTER HAD A TOY HOUSE. I LOVED GOING HOME WITH HIM AND PLAYING WITH HIS TOYS, (WE HAD VERY FEW TOYS). I GOT MANY WHIPPINGS FOR NOT COMING STRAIGHT HOME FROM SCHOOL. ALSO WENT TO MILDRED'S HOUSE A LOT. SHE LIVED IN TOWN TOO AND HER DAD OWNED THE GROCERY STORE.

This colorful background paper creates a lively context for this single photograph and journal block. The photo and patriotic paper support Mother's journal account of starting her one-room-school day with the Pledge of Allegiance.

A stamp pad was used to dye the vellum under Mother's journaling and tearing the edges of the text block made it look like an old document.

Learn everything you possibly can, and you will discover later that none of it was superfluous. — Hugh of St. Victor

Behold, children are a heritage from the Lord . . . — Psalm 127:3

Time

School Days

1922

School days, school days
Dear old golden rule days.
Readin' and writin' and 'rithmetic
Taught to the tune of a hickory stick.
You were my queen in calico
I was your bashful, barefoot beau
And I wrote on your slate
"I love you so"
when we were a couple of kids.
— Unknown

Supplies List

Paper: K & Company
Cardstock: Memories Forever/Westrim Crafts
Vellum: Paper Garden
Stickers: The Okie-Dokie Press
Lettering: QuicKutz
Dye pad: Memories/Sand, Stewart Superior Corporation
Computer font: Pyxid Condensed, The Print Shop/Broderbund

But the excellence of knowledge is that wisdom
gives life to those who have it. — Ecclesiastes 7:12

WE BEGIN AND END WITH FAMILY

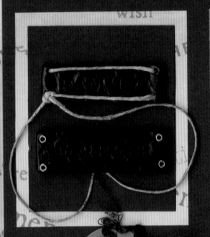

I am the tallest child in the front row. Brother Vernon is on my right and Doris, who came to live with us after her mother died, is on my left. Dad is behind Vernon and Mom is behind Doris. Notice the black stockings that I have never liked. I don't remember the reason for this picture ... but family was always important to us.

Keep scale in mind when you want to feature a single photo on a two-page layout. Enlarge your photos and text so they become more significant. Use 3-dimensional embellishments for more impact.

Family ties are precious bonds
That passing time endears,
For they begin with memories,
Of our happy childhood years.
— Unknown

What we call the beginning is so often the end.
And to make an end is to make a beginning;
the end is where we start from.
— T.S. Eliot

He has made everything beautiful in its time;
*Also He has put eternity in their hearts, except that no one
can find out the work that God does from beginning to end.*
— *Ecclesiastes 3:11*

But as for me and my house, we will serve the Lord. — *Joshua 24:15*

A family is a little world created by love. — *Unknown*

Supplies List

Paper:	Design Originals; Mulberry Paper by PSX
Cardstock:	Bazzill Basics Paper
Stickers:	Inspirables™ Stone Stickers (EK Success); Ever After Scrapbook Co.; Colorbök
Metal tiles and dots:	Scrapyard 329
Dotlets:	doodlebug design, inc.
Metal Coin:	Darice, Inc.
Page Pebbles:	Making Memories
Fiber:	American Hemp
Computer Fonts:	2Peas Composition and 2PeasHot Chocolate from twopeasinabucket.com

We do not remember days.
We remember the moments.

All of the papers used in the album were purchased before this project was begun. You will probably buy specific papers to match the mood and era of your personal images. I selected photos to go with my papers and often used dye pads to coordinate colors.

This charming floral pattern works because it is similar to the fabrics used for little girls' dresses of this time period. Coordinated flower stickers and borders created an attractive finish to the page bottoms. It was necessary however, to design page-top corners to balance the heavier visual weight of the floral borders at the bottom.

I had long hair and wore huge hair ribbons until I was about 9 years old. Then I got a dutch boy cut. Hair cuts were 25 cents in 1926. On June 12, 1926, we were blessed with a baby brother. I was 9 years old. Vern was 6 and Frieda was 3. Mom and dad named him Carl Jr. after my dad. We called him "Carlie".

Beloved, now we are children of God; and it has not yet been revealed what we shall be, but we know that when He is revealed, we shall be like Him, for we shall see Him as He is. — 1 John 3:2

Memories are bouquets tied with heart strings. — Unknown

The love in our family flows strong and deep, leaving us memories to treasure and keep. — Unknown

Supplies List

Paper:	Daisy D's Paper Company
Cardstock:	Paper Garden
Texting paper:	K & Company
Stickers, borders, frame cutouts:	K & Company
Dye pad:	Memories/Sand, Stewart Superior Corporation
Punch:	Anna Griffin
Title:	Paper Pizazz by Hot Off The Press
Computer font:	Scogin, The Print Shop/Broderbund

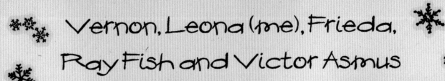

Vernon, Leona (me), Frieda,
Ray Fish and Victor Asmus

For my 9th birthday party my mom invited the gang out for a party. She made cake, ice cream and double fudge. We played games and dad hitched the horses to a sleigh and put the sleigh bells on, filled the sleigh with straw and on a clear moonlit, snow crested night, took us for a ride. We sang all the way. He then took them all home. No one wanted to go first.

An obvious background choice for winter photos would be snow patterned papers. The background chosen here is reminiscent of the warm flannel clothing and handmade quilts that would be used to ward off winter's chill after a day on "Sleigh Ride Hill". Choose less predictable combinations for dynamic layouts. The font and stickers used here convey an appropriate childlike playfulness.

Memories are like a patchwork quilt . . . each section is sewn together to wrap around us for comfort and warmth in the years to come. — Unknown

A family is a patchwork of love. — Unknown

Sleigh Ride Hill

The girls and women would wear long bloomers with elastic at the knee. For winter, they were made of flannel. I remember going to school with long johns. When I got older I didn't want any one to see them around my ankles with long stockings over them. So when we got over the hill, I would stop and roll them up above my knees and on the way home, I'd roll them down again so my parents couldn't chew me out. By the way the long stockings were often black ribbed cotton.

In winter we would all meet at the top of Sleigh Ride Hill with our sleds. We even rode in metal bushel baskets. Had a few toboggans. There were about 12 or 15 of us enjoying the snow. Then there was the ice on our creek where we went ice skating in our shoes. My brother did make me a pair of shoes skates from a pair of his shoes. We painted them red.

A family is pieced together with hope and faith. — Unknown

A merry heart does good like medicine. — Proverbs 17:22

Families are like quilts . . .
Lives pieced together,
Stitched with smiles and tears,
Colored with each memory,
And bound with love and prayers. — Unknown

Supplies List

Paper:	The Paper Loft LLC
Cardstock:	Bazzill Basics Paper
	Mulberry Paper by PSX
Stickers:	The Okie-Dokie Press
Dye pad:	Memories/Sand, Stewart Superior Corporation
Die cut:	Sign Post, Sizzix/Ellison/Provo Craft
Punch:	Snowflake, Marvy Uchida
Chalk:	Craf-T Products
Computer font:	CB Brush Strokes, The Journaling Genie™
	Chatterbox® (EK Success)

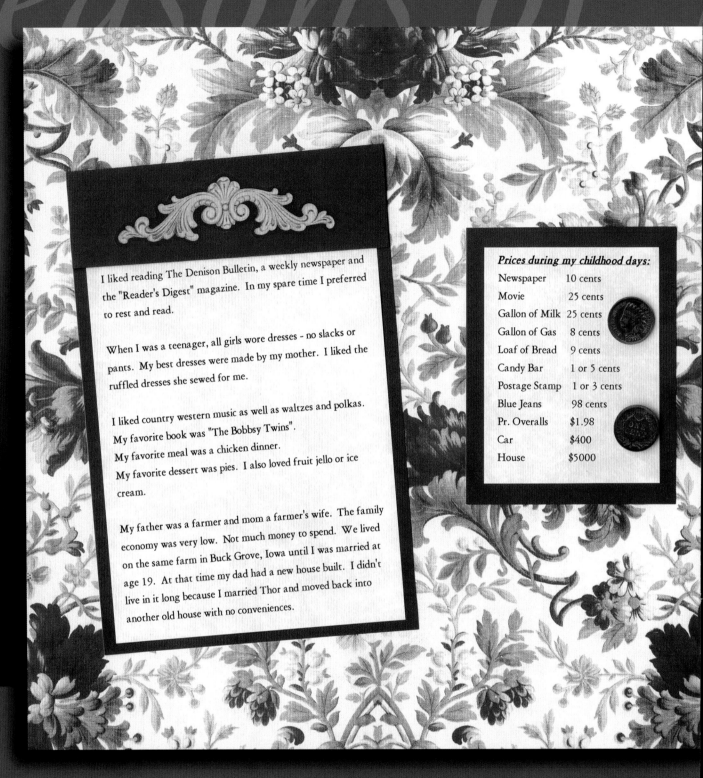

I liked reading The Denison Bulletin, a weekly newspaper and the "Reader's Digest" magazine. In my spare time I preferred to rest and read.

When I was a teenager, all girls wore dresses - no slacks or pants. My best dresses were made by my mother. I liked the ruffled dresses she sewed for me.

I liked country western music as well as waltzes and polkas.
My favorite book was "The Bobbsy Twins".
My favorite meal was a chicken dinner.
My favorite dessert was pies. I also loved fruit jello or ice cream.

My father was a farmer and mom a farmer's wife. The family economy was very low. Not much money to spend. We lived on the same farm in Buck Grove, Iowa until I was married at age 19. At that time my dad had a new house built. I didn't live in it long because I married Thor and moved back into another old house with no conveniences.

Prices during my childhood days:

Newspaper	10 cents
Movie	25 cents
Gallon of Milk	25 cents
Gallon of Gas	8 cents
Loaf of Bread	9 cents
Candy Bar	1 or 5 cents
Postage Stamp	1 or 3 cents
Blue Jeans	98 cents
Pr. Overalls	$1.98
Car	$400
House	$5000

A "notepad" was created for Mother's journal block by folding down the top edge of a burgundy paper. This created a support for the sticker that repeats the gray tones of the photo opposite promoting unity in these pages.

Imagine how lifeless this layout would be in a traditional black photo album. Using vibrant tones and pattern on occasion will energize your design and entice the viewer to linger.

But as for me, I trust in You, O Lord;
I say, "You are my God.
My times are in Your hand . . . — Psalm 31:14, 15

Leona(me), Helen Frey, Esther Meyer, Nellie Nolan, Dorothy Nance, Jessie Unland, Doris Tinnemann (cousin) and Frieda, my sister.

My little children, let us not love in word or in tongue, but in deed and in truth. — John 3:18

We are shaped and fashioned by what we love. — Goethe.

After the friendship of God, a friend's affection is the greatest treasure here below. — Unknown

Good friends, good books and a sleepy conscience: this is the ideal life. — Mark Twain

Supplies List

Paper : Anna Griffin
Stickers: Ever After Scrapbook Co.
Frame: Colorbök
Punch: Anna Griffin
Lace border: Fiskars Photo Memory Accents/Fiskars Brands, Inc.
Other: Indian head pennies
Computer font: Amery, The Print Shop/Broderbund

The embellishments and stickers used on the far left and right of these pages balance each other asymmetrically and use repetition of color and texture to create unity.

The cream and floral background paper mimics the dress fabric Mother used to sew the girls' dresses. Chalk and a cotton swab were used to tint the torn green paper edges and match the adjacent cream colors.

Family ties are precious threads no matter where we roam.
They draw us close to those we love and pull our hearts toward home.
— Unknown

1929

DRESSES

This is a picture of Carlie, Dat, Doris and me (Leona). Dat and Doris are wearing dresses that I made for them.

She makes tapestry for herself;
Her clothing is fine linen and purple. — Proverbs 31:22

To accomplish great things, we must not only act, but also dream; not only plan, but also believe.
— Anatole France

Supplies List

Paper :	Daisy D's Paper Company; Mini Graphics; SEI
Stickers:	Colorbök
Buttons:	Dress It Up, Jesse James and Company
Ribbon:	Magic Scraps
Lettering:	QuicKutz
Corner rounder punch:	Marvy Uchida
Majestic corner punch:	Fiskars Brands, Inc.
Computer font:	Papyrus, (Internet)

A family stitched together with love seldom unravels. — Unknown

CHILDHOOD

The objects from Mother's childhood that rest on this "shelf" were scanned
and printed on photo paper. Most often when someone dies, their possessions are
distributed throughout the family. Scanning and printing copies of these precious
objects allows each person in that family a visual replica of the heirloom.

TIME TREASURES

Marker was used to create the vertical lines which imitate wainscoting under the lace trimmed "shelf". A marker was also used to create a cast shadow of the lace and develop more depth.

*To everything there is a season,
a time for every purpose under heaven.*
— Ecclesiastes 3:1

Supplies List

Paper: Daisy D's Paper Company
Stickers: Nostalgiques™ by Rebecca Sower Designs (EK Success); K & Company
Lettering: QuicKutz
Frame: The Print Shop/Broderbund

I am a miser of my memories of you and will not spend them. — *Witter Bynner*

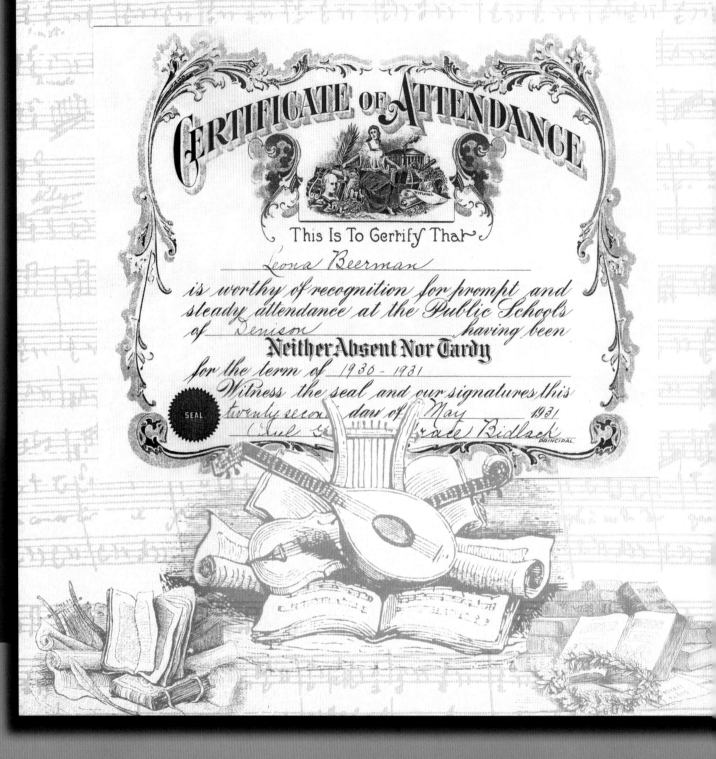

CERTIFICATE OF ATTENDANCE

This Is To Certify That

Leona Beerman

is worthy of recognition for prompt and steady attendance at the Public Schools of *Denison* having been

Neither Absent Nor Tardy

for the term of *1930 - 1931*

Witness the seal and our signatures this twenty second day of *May* 1931

SEAL

Grace Bidlack
PRINCIPAL

The musical instruments in the background paper were cut to overlap the certificate and photo. The class photo was then glued along three sides to the background, producing a pocket for Mother's graduation memorabilia.

Go confidently in the direction of your dreams.
Live the life you've imagined.
— Henry David Thoreau

Curiosity is one of the permanent and certain characteristics of a vigorous mind.
— Samuel Johnson

Eighth Grade Graduation
Crawford County Schools
August 15, 1930
1:30 P. M.
Opera House
Denison, Iowa

DENISON PUBLIC SCHOOLS

But also for this very reason, giving all diligence, add to your faith virtue,
to virtue knowledge, to knowledge self-control, to self-control perseverance,
to perseverance godliness, to godliness brotherly kindness,
and to brotherly kindness love.
— 2 Peter 1:5, 6, 7

Education is not filling a pail but the lighting of a fire.
— William Butler Yeats

Supplies List

Paper: The Family Archives LLC
Other: Scanned certificate, photo and programs.

When the world says, "Give up,"
Hope whispers, "Try it one more time." — Unknown

I had confirmation classes every morning at the Parochial Lutheran School in Denison, Ia, taught by Pastor Frese for an hour. Then Leona and I had to walk or run across town, about a mile, to the high school. It was hard enough adjusting from country school to high school and coming in an hour late didn't help matters any. But it worked out as everything finally does. I was confirmed on Palm Sunday in March 29, 1931 with a class of 45. I was asked only 3 questions. This was in the Denison Zion Lutheran Church. Dad bought me an expensive white dress and white shoes and I wore a carnation corsage. I had pictures taken at the studio. Uncle Bill and Aunt Gladys came out from Omaha for the occasion. We were all at Grandma Beermann's in Denison that Sunday along with Leora Bruns' family.

Monochromatic color schemes have become very popular and are a great way to develop harmony in design.

The journaling was typed on light colored paper then topped with tinted vellum to mimic the collage-style background paper.

The spiritual life does not remove us from the world but leads us deeper into it. — Henri J. Nouwen

Feed your faith and your fears will starve to death. — Unknown

Try using small frames inside a photo to develop special emphasis. These frames may be punched or hand cut from paper or cardstock.

In faith there is enough light for those who want to believe and enough shadows to blind those who don't. — Blaise Pascal

Supplies List

Paper: Paper Pizazz by Hot Off The Press
Stickers: Stickopotamus® (EK Success)
Vellum: Paper Pizazz by Hot Off The Press
Cardstock: Paper Garden
Computer font: Notehand, The Print Shop/Broderbund

L
ESTHER
O
N
A

I had a bosom friend. Her name was Esther Meyer. We were always together for years and years; from childhood through Junior High School.

This green background paper reminded me of a fabric that might have been used for a winter coat worn in mom's day.

I created an acrostic of Mother's and Esther's names to display how close they had been much of their lives. The tree, now barren of leaves, seems to represent the ebbing of their friendship as described in her journal.

Like branches on a tree, we may grow in different directions,
yet our roots remain as one. Each of our lives will always be a special part of the other.
— Unknown

As children, we played together most of the time either at her house or my house. We would play house in our empty corn crib. We even went to the barn and got some eggs the hens laid to put in our mud pies. Mom didn't know about this.

There were other friends like Helma, Della, Helen, Anita, Nellie and Irene, but Esther and I were really close. Dad bought me a real classy graduation dress because I liked it and wanted it. Our class had their picture taken on the Court House lawn. Aug 15, 1930. Esther and I had our picture taken on the steps alone too. Dad didn't really want me to go to high school. I begged and he finally consented.

My friend Esther didn't go to high school so I didn't see as much of her any more. She went out to California and stayed there until she retired. Then she came back to Denison , Iowa with her family. She never married. I go to see her every time I'm in Denison . We still have good memories.

But his delight is in the law of the LORD;
and in his law he meditates day and night.
He shall be like a tree planted by the rivers of water,
that brings forth its fruit in its season,
whose leaf also shall not wither;
and whatever he does shall prosper.
— Psalm 1:2, 3

The most beautiful discovery true friends make
is that they can grow separately without growing apart.
— Elisabeth Foley

Supplies List

Paper: Rocky Mountain Scrapbook Company
Stickers: Karen Foster Design
Die cut: Autumn Tree, 3-012, Deluxe Design LLC ©
Cutouts: Fresh Cuts ™ Printed Accents by Rebecca Sower Designs (EK Success); This and That Alphabets; My Mind's Eye, Inc.
Dye pad: Memories/Sand, Stewart Superior Corporation
Computer fonts: Journal (Internet); 2 Peas Fudge Brownie from twopeasinabucket.com

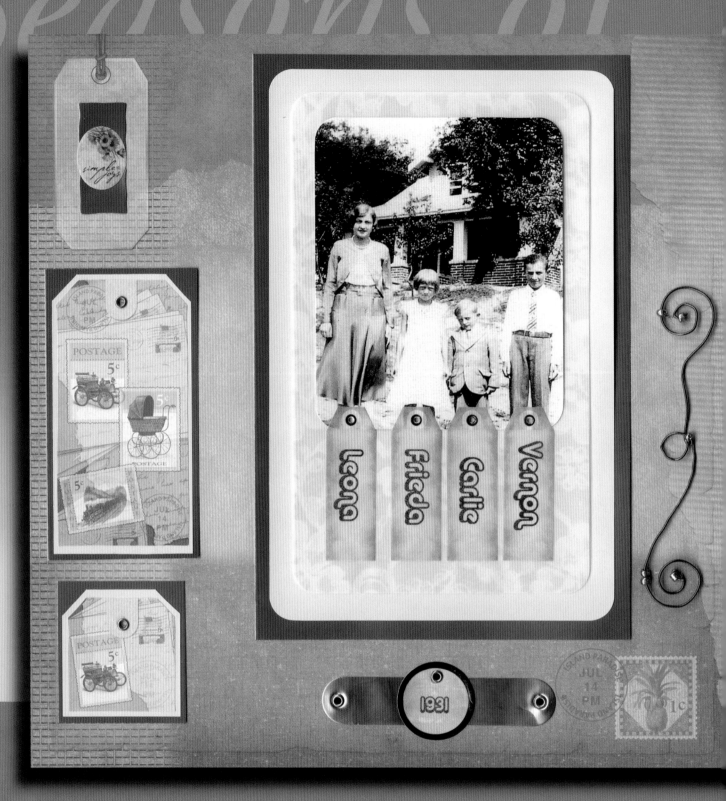

The use of metal here inspired a new color scheme. Copper strips, wire, eyelets, beads and copper paper make this layout cohesive and interesting.

Note how the complementary tones of "red and green" create energy on these pages. Mother and her siblings are photographed in front of their newly finished home from which she would soon travel. The background paper, tags and postcards anticipate this new passage.

Notice the torn papers behind the postcard which repeat the irregular edges of the collage-style background paper.

Trust in the Lord with all your heart, And lean not on your own understanding;
In all your ways acknowledge Him, And He shall direct your paths. — Proverbs 3:5, 6

GREETINGS SINCERE

Whether you use a steel pen,
or a quill,
Not a jot does it matter to me,
It's not how you write,
But the words you indite,
Makes me anxious your writing
to see.

New Home

SIBLINGS

Supplies List

Paper: Paper Pizazz by Hot Off The Press	*Tags:* Paper Pizazz by Hot Off The Press
Patterned vellum: Autumn Leaves	*Dye pad:* Memories/Sand, Stewart Superior Corporation
Cardstock: Paper Garden	*Other:* Post card from Mother's collection, copper strip tags
Lettering: QuicKutz	*Computer font:* Alba Super (Internet)
Sticker tags: Stickopotamus® (EK Success)	
Wire: Artistic Wire	
Corner punch: Marvy Uchida	
Eyelets: Making Memories	
Poemstones: Sonnets, Creative Imaginations	

Traveling is not just seeing the new; it is also leaving behind.
Not just opening doors; also closing them behind you, never to return.
But the place you have left forever is always there for you to see
whenever you shut your eyes. — Jan Myrdal

The plaid of the background paper used here relates to the dresses in this photo and compliments the tones in the autograph book. Notice how all objects but the "plaids" have curvilinear lines, which set them apart from the background.

A soft font shadow was created to subtly repeat some tones in the autograph pages.

The flower above the hearts was retrieved from the border punches. Save and file your punch clippings for other layouts.

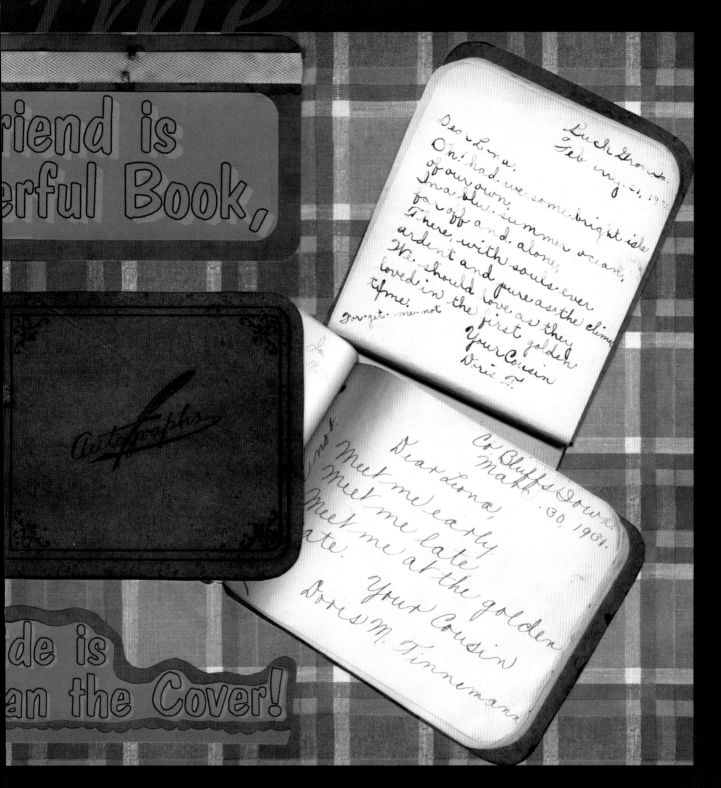

riend is

erful Book,

de is

an the Cover!

Finally, brethren, whatever things are true, whatever things are noble, whatever things are just, whatever things are pure, whatever things are lovely, whatever things are of good report, if there is any virtue and if there is anything praiseworthy — meditate on these things. **— Philippians 4:8**

Being deeply loved by someone gives you strength, while loving someone deeply gives you courage. **— Tao Tzu**

Supplies List

Paper:	Rocky Mountain Scrapbook Company, Daisy D's Paper Company
Cardstock:	Bazzill Basics Paper
Charm:	Source unknown
Punch:	Fiskars Brands, Inc.
Corner punch:	Marvy Uchida
Dye pad:	Memories/Sand, Stewart Superior Corporation
Other:	Scanned autograph book, twill, wire and beads sources unknown
Computer font:	Franciscan, The Print Shop/Broderbund

My cousin Doris from Omaha stayed with us most of the time. Her mother died when she was 2 years old. She was a sister to us and we shared our mom and dad with her. We all liked horse back riding. We rode very well. Dad had gentle horses so we could all ride. One day I rode one of the horses to my Aunt Martha's place. She, the horse, got tired of me on her back, so she went under a low limb on a tree and brushed me off.

When we were old enough, we all had our cows to milk, night and morning; also chickens to feed and eggs to gather. The boys would feed the pigs and give hay to the cows and water the horses. We had a hand turned separator that would separate the cream form the milk. One day Doris and I were going to spend the day with my cousins who lived 5 miles away. We got up at daybreak and milked 13 cows, then mounted our horses and rode away. Our cousins were our age and we had a grand time with them. Their mother always had pie for us besides the good meals. This day a storm came up while we were riding home. It rained so hard we had to stop at a farm place. Mr. Fitzpatrick took our horses and told us to go into the house. They asked us to stay for supper. We had fried potatoes and Doris didn't get a fork to eat with and wouldn't ask for one. We had such beautiful rainbows after the rains. Several families of cousins use to come and stay with us, sometimes for a week. My Grandfather Beermann use to live with us for a time too. He wood make wine in our cellar. He put it in jugs and corked them. I even got to sleep with him at times. My dad's older brother who was single, use to live with us too. He helped dad with the work. I some times wonder how mom got all the cooking and baking done. When Uncle Herman didn't live with us, dad would hire a man to help out, make the hay into huge stacks, mow the weeds, cut the grain and thrash it, pick corn by hand and unload it by scooping it up into the crib. Mom helped with corn picking and grain cutting and shocking.

It was hot and dry during the summer and not much feed for the cattle so dad had us herd the cattle along the roadsides so they could eat the grass. We had to keep them corralled so they wouldn't go too far. Time got long. We braided dandelions, pulled apart snake grass played with milkweed flowers and pods and teased beetles and other bugs, when we weren't chasing cows. Some days, we walked all through the cornfields hoeing cockleburs. We would take about 3 or 4 rows at a time. There was never a dull moment on the farm. We had a big garden and a big patch of potatoes. We picked up bushels and bushels of potatoes, brought them in by the wagonload and stored them in the cellar. Also had an apple orchard and lots of apples to pick.

The old adage, "A picture is worth a thousand words" may be true, but in my scrapbooking experience, words greatly enhance a photo. Here, Mom's words gently evoke many images of an era that has passed.

But a woman who fears the Lord, she shall be praised.
Give her of the fruit of her hands, and let her own works praise her in the gates.
— Proverbs 31:30, 31

I learned this, at least, by my experiment: that if one advances confidently in the direction of his dreams, and endeavors to live the life which he has imagined, he will meet with a success unexpected in common hours.
— Henry David Thoreau

Riding at Bertram's in Ireton, Iowa - 1932

On this page, a torn, rolled and "stitched" framework of paper emphasizes Mother's portrait. This rather rugged framing technique contrasts the feminine presence I always associated with her. Mom wore dresses on the farm even when riding a horse, mowing the lawn, driving the tractor or feeding the chickens.

Supplies List

Paper:	Rocky Mountain Scrapbook Company; Paper Adventures; SEI
Cardstock:	Bazzill Basics Paper
Paper ribbon:	Unknown
Twine:	American Hemp
Metal squares:	Scrapyard 329
Computer font:	Pepita MT, Poor Richard (Internet)

BROOK'S

PATENT GLACÉ & SOFT MACHINE COTTON

CROCHET & EMBROIDERY

FIRST PREMIUM

SECOND PREMIUM

Crawford County
Shortcourse &
4-H
Club Fair
IOWA

Crawford County
Shortcourse &
4-H
Club Fair
IOWA

The Lucky 4-H club girls received seventeen prizes on their sewing which they exhibited in Denison last Saturday. Erma Carstens received eight prizes, Leona Beermann five, Irene Stover three, and Della Theobald one. They were all very well satisfied.

PLEASE REPORT TO

4-H Club Office

West end of Grandstand
Fair Grounds

Tuesday - 5:15 P.M.

August 29, 1933.

Miss Leona Beermann

4-H

Souvenir
Des Moines
Iowa

Iowa
State Fair

Buck Grove, Iowa, June 5, 1933. The Lucky 4-H club met at the Stover school house on June 2d, with eight members present. The following officers were elected: Leader, Mrs. Henry Bumann; assistant leader, Mrs. William Carstens; president, Irma Carstens; vice president, Irene Stover; secretary and treasurer, Leona Beermann; reporter, Esther Meyer. The program committee was also elected. Irma Carstens served refreshments. The next meeting will be held at the home of Irene Stover on June 22d.

BOYS' AND GIRLS' DINING HALL
IOWA STATE FAIR
1933
MEAL TICKET
(Good only for meals not cancelled)

4-H was a big part of Mother's younger years. She had accumulated so much

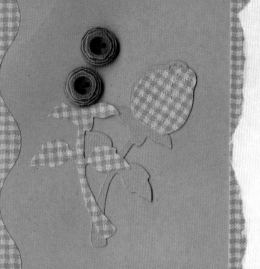

For many years I was a member of the Washington Twp. Lucky 4-H club. We learned sewing, cooking and baking bread. In August of 1933 I was chosen the Crawford County Health Winner at the State Fair. Horace Westcott was the healthiest boy. We spent several days at the fair attending State Health Champion's luncheons and more. This was at age 16. The same year, I was elected the County Vice President of the 4-H clubs.

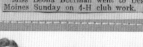

Miss Leona Beerman went to Des Moines Sunday on 4-H club work.

See how the gingham paper is used on all four pages to develop continuity when displaying many different objects. Be playful in your designs by doing the unexpected. Notice the homey irregular stitching around the group photo that would never have appeared in Mother's work.

Supplies List

Paper:	Daisy D's Paper Company
Cardstock:	Bazzill Basics Paper
Flower die cut:	Sizzix/Ellison/Provo Craft
Wave template:	Custom Cutting System:12-inch Pattern, Creative Memories
Ad image:	The Print Shop/Broderbund
Other:	Buttons, fair ribbons and scanned objects
Computer font:	Typewriter (Internet)

CONTINUE ➤

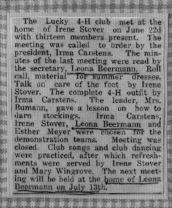

The Lucky 4-H club met at the home of Irene Stover on June 22d with thirteen members present. The meeting was called to order by the president, Irma Carstens. The minutes of the last meeting were read by the secretary, Leona Beermann. Roll call, material for summer dresses. Talk on care of the feet by Irene Stover. The complete 4-H outfit by Irma Carstens. The leader, Mrs. Rumann, gave a lesson on how to darn stockings. Irma Carstens, Irene Stover, Leona Beermann and Esther Meyer were chosen for the demonstration teams. Meeting was closed. Club songs and club dancing were practiced, after which refreshments were served by Irene Stover and Mary Wingrove. The next meeting will be held at the home of Leona Beermann on July 13th.

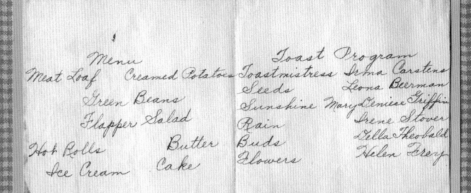

Menu
Meat Loaf   Creamed Potatoes
Green Beans
Flapper Salad
Hot Rolls   Butter
Ice Cream   Cake

Toast Program
Toastmistress   Irma Carstens
Seeds   Leona Beerman
Sunshine   Mary Deniece Griffin
Rain   Irene Stover
Buds   Zella Theobald
Flowers   Helen Frey

Lucky 4-H
Banquet

Buck Grove, Iowa, July 17, 1933.
The Lucky 4-H club met at the home of Leona Beermann July 13th, with the leader and nineteen members present. The meeting was called to order by the president, Erma Carstens. Roll call: Name the different parts of a sewing machine. The minutes of the last meeting were read by the secretary, Leona Beermann. Talk, Threading and adjustment of a sewing machine. How to clean white shoes by each member. Meeting adjourned, after which club songs were practiced. Refreshments were served by Leona Beermann and Annette Ludeman. The next meeting will be held at the home of Denice Griffin, July 27th.

4-H
Banquet
1929

Leona Beerman

Most of the items on these pages and on the two previous pages were copied
from the scrapbook Mom made as a teenager. Her buttons and tracer wheel
were scanned to avoid adding bulk to the pages. Notice how the black
background seems to add more depth to the 3-dimensional articles.

*And Jesus said to them, "I am the bread of life. He who comes to Me shall never
hunger, and he who believes in Me shall never thirst." — John 6:35*

Whenever you are sincerely pleased you are nourished. — Ralph Waldo Emerson

MARGARET DUNHAM
HEADS 4-H GIRLS

**SHE WILL REPRESENT CRAW-
FORD COUNTY AT
STATE FAIR.**

Special to The Nonpareil.
DENISON, Aug. 27. —Margaret
Dunham was elected president of
the Crawford county 4-H members
at an achievement program this
week.
She was named also, the style
show winner and will represent the
county at the state fair.
Other officers elected are Leona
Beermann, vice president; Opal
Yankey, secretary and treasurer,
and Irene Plover, historian.
The 4-H boys had over 100 ex-
hibits entered in the program.

*Cheerfulness keeps up a kind of daylight in the mind
and fills it with a steady and perpetual serenity.*
— Joseph Addison

If you have knowledge, let others light their candles at it. — Margaret Fuller

Manners easily and rapidly mature into morals. — Horace Mann

Supplies List

Paper: Daisy D's Paper Company;
Anna Griffin
Cardstock: Bazzill Basics Paper
Postcard and sewing machine images: The Print Shop/Broderbund
Other: Scanned items from
Mother's scrapbook

Scrapbook from youth.

LEONA

This Ticket and 10 Cents
Will Admit One person to
Harr Brothers Show
On Date Advertised Here

*Tent Show in Buck Grove
She went with Bruns and
left Frieda home in the
Back House*

GOOD FOR
ONE GAME OF GOLF
AT THE
DENISON JUNIOR COUNTRY CLUB
Finest and Sportiest Miniature
Golf Course in the Middle West
WELL LIGHTED NIGHTS WITH 40 FLOOD LIGHTS

ONE BLOCK NORTH OF POSTOFFICE
VOID AFTER JULY 1, 1931

*Helma + I wore our pajamas
to Denison. Each got free
golf ticket.*

MOTOR
ABILITY
TESTS

CRAWFORD
COUNTY
SCHOOLS

DENISON, IOWA
MAY, 1930

FREE! FREE! FREE!
This Merchant Ticket and One Paid Adult Admission
WILL ADMIT TWO PERSONS
RIALTO THEATRE
Monday, Wednesday and Friday Evenings Only
(Except Holidays)
Good Until NOV 1 1932
SIOUX CITY'S FAMILY THEATRE

*From Sioux City, Iowa
the time I was there
August 1932.*

These pages display Mother's active social life as chronicled in her personal scrapbook. She constructed a scrapbook cover from heavy cardboard, wrapped it with cloth and bound it with two ring fasteners. Some sections were scanned that included Mother's own handwriting to bring special visual meaning to the reader.

For with You is the fountain of life; In Your light we see light. — *Psalm 36:9*

Not knowing when the dawn will come, I open every door. — *Emily Dickinson*

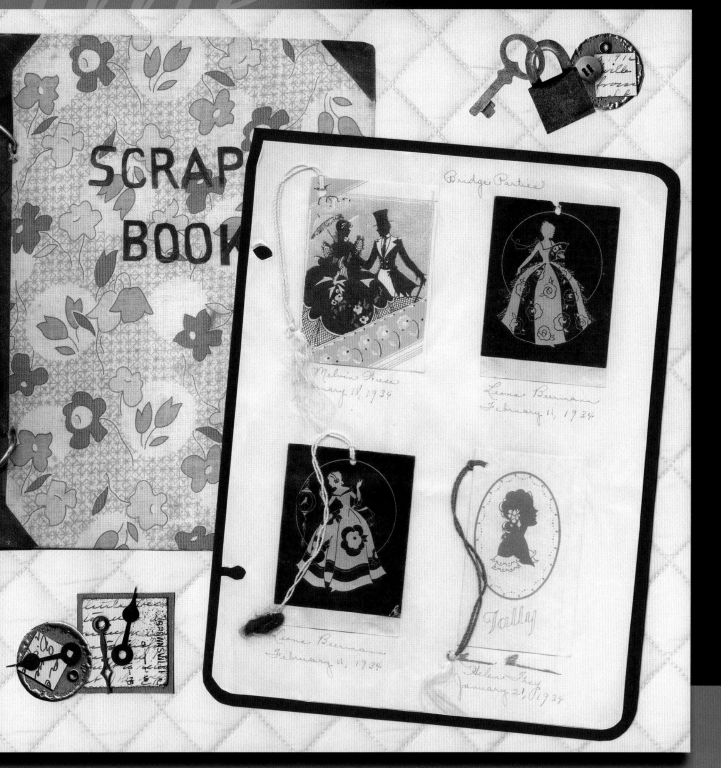

If you can walk, you can dance. If you can talk, you can sing.
— *Zimbabwe Proverb*

But I have called you friends, for all things that I heard from My Father I have made known to you.
— *John 15:15*

There is just one life for each of us; our own. — *Euripides*

Supplies List

Paper:	K & Company
Cardstock:	Bazzill Basics Paper
Brad stickers:	Creative Imaginations
Stickers:	Nostalgiques™ by Rebecca Sower Designs (EK Success); key and padlock by Karen Foster Design
Clock hands:	Fresh Cuts™ Printed Accents by Rebecca Sower Designs (EK Success)
Brads:	Magic Scraps
Other:	Scanned objects
Computer font:	Bottled Farts (Internet)

Page 55

Leora and I masquerading as a bride and groom. The bride, Leora, is wearing my mother's old wedding veil.

The brown tiles spaced horizontally across the middle of this pre-printed paper inspired me to make windows to feature the title. An "H" cut was made in the vellum to create "shutters". The exposed brown areas provided a frame for the die cut letters, which blend nicely with the softly rendered design.

If you want to live more, you must master the art of appreciating the little everyday blessings of life. This is not altogether a golden work, but there are countless gleams of gold to be discovered in it.
— *Henry Alford Porter*

Carl
Vernon
Me
Frieda

YOUTH

To create a different affect, place a photo under vellum.
This softens and adds a bit of mystery to the layout.

Three grand essentials to happiness in this life are
something to do, something to love, and something to hope for.
— Joseph Addison

Therefore my heart is glad, and my glory rejoices;
my flesh also will rest in hope. — Psalm 16:9

And now, Lord, what do I want for? My hope is in You. — Psalm 39:7

Supplies List

Paper: The Paper Loft LLC; SEI
Vellum: Autumn Leaves
Bronze eyelets: Making Memories
Lettering: QuicKutz
Other: Metal coins, ribbon
Computer font: Bickley Script (Internet)

This picture was taken a month before
my wedding in front of the new house
my dad had built.

The inspiration for this layout came from the black print paper with small rust colored flowers. The elegant marble paper in rust makes a sassy background for the stylish hats, dresses and shoes. This seemed to make a fashion statement characteristic of my mother.

Eloquence lies as much in the tone of the voice,
in the eyes, and in the speaker's manner,
as in his choice of words.
— La Rochefoucauld

One thing I have desired of the Lord,
That will I seek:
That I may dwell in the house of the Lord
All the days of my life,
To behold the beauty of the Lord . . . — Psalm 27:4

Life is no brief candle to me.
It is a sort of splendid torch
which I have got ahold of
for the moment,
and I want to make it burn
as brightly as possible
before handing it on to
future generations.

—George Bernard Shaw

Me and my mom, Lena Beermann

A man can not be comfortable without his own approval. — *Mark Twain*

Consider the lilies, how they grow: they neither toil nor spin; and yet I say to you, even Solomon in all his glory was not arrayed like one of these. If then God so clothes the grass, which today is in the field and tomorrow is thrown into the oven, how much more will He clothe you, O you of little faith? — *Luke 12:27, 28*

Supplies List

Paper:	Paper Pizazz by Hot Off The Press; The Paper Loft LLC
Stickers:	Colorbök
Cutouts:	Fresh Cuts™ Printed Accents by Rebecca Sower Designs (EK Success)
Words of Wisdom:	Paper Pizazz by Hot Off The Press
Punch:	Fiskars Brands, Inc.
Computer font:	Alps (Internet)

Senior Class of 1934
Denison High School

Leona Beerman	Marval Keller
Ninette Boettger	Elmer Koeppen
Russell Bray	Arlene Kropf
Mary Byers	Viola Kropf
Elnora Carlson	Irene Kruse
Billy Carlyle	LaVonne Lee
Irma Carstens	Blaine Lilleholm
Thomas Collins	Gerald Lovejoy
Jim Conner	Roy Lundquist
Chester Cramer	Joe Malloy
Gerald Dannels	Helen Marquardt
Zelmon Day	Russell Mesenbrink
Margaret Evers	Emil Moeller
Kathryn Ewall	Clarence Mueller
Evelyn Finnegan	Fairy Nelson
Gaylord Foderberg	Vera Pautsch
Irma Frahm	Stanley Pester
Carl Frese	Lucille Podey
Helen Goebel	Ruth Powell
Clarion Green	Jim Ransom
Wilbur Grill	Rex Rogers
Gailen Hain	Jack Saggau
Maurice Henkin	Fern Shives
Warner Henney	Paul Stapleton
Fredrick Hoffman	Harold Stender
Carey Houlihan	Elizabeth Suntken
Esther Huebner	Lois Towne
Paul Hultsch	Allison Waldron
Kenneth Hutchinson	Donald Weiss
Marvin Jedele	Horace Westcott
George Johnson	Billy Wheeler
Clarion Keating	Alberta Wiese
Elizabeth Keating	Melvin Wiese
	Helen Wigg

CLASS OFFICERS:—

President _____Roy Lundquist
Vice-President _____Mary Byers
Secretary _____Ninette Boettger
Treasurer _____Gerald Dannels

ACTIVITIES:—

May 9 _____Junior-Senior Banquet
May 18 _____School Exhibit at Gym (afternoon and evening)
May 20 _____Baccalaureate Services at Gymnasium,
Rev. C. S. Carroll, speaker.
May 22 _____Senior Class Play
May 24 _____Commencement Exercises at Gymnasium
H. E. Bradford of University of Nebraska, speaker.

The diagonal paper used in this layout adds elegance and energy to an otherwise quiet and straightforward topic.

If one advances confidently in the direction of his dreams, and endeavors to live the life, which he has imagined, he will meet with a success unexpected in common hours. — Henry David Thoreau

I know not what the future holds, but I know who holds the future. — Unknown

The invariable mark of wisdom is to see the miraculous in the common. — Ralph Waldo Emerson

1934

LEONA

The ability to perceive the significance of the small things of the world
is the secret of clear sightedness.
The guarding of what is soft and vulnerable is the secret of strength.
— Unknown

Cut not the wings of your dreams, for they are the heartbeat
and the freedom of your soul. — Flavia

I press toward the goal for the prize of the upward call of God in Christ Jesus.
— Philippians 3:14

Supplies List

Paper: NRN Designs; The Crafter's Workshop;
The Family Archives LLC
Lettering: QuicKutz
Other: Scanned newsprint

Only your heart can tell you what is precious. Only your heart can tell you what is precious.

The Future
Belongs to Those
Who Believe in
the Beauty
of Their
Dreams.
– Eleanor Roosevelt

Diploma

The embossed design elements of Mom's diploma cover influenced choosing this background paper. The foliage surrounding "Diploma" and the narrow stripes above and below the word recur in the floral pattern.

The font printed on vellum takes center stage in this two-page layout and was chosen to match what was printed on the original document.

It isn't how little you know that matters, but how anxious you are to learn. — *C. Newland*

Seek to know the truth, but above all, love Truth. — *Unknown*

Only your heart can tell you what is precious. Only your heart can tell you what is precious.

Senior High School
Denison, Iowa
This is to Certify that

Leona E. Beermann

having completed the Course of Study, as prescribed by the Board of Education, is declared a Graduate of the Senior High School, and is therefore awarded this

Diploma

In Witness Whereof, our signatures are hereunto affixed.

Given at Denison, Iowa, this 24th day of May 1934

C.E. Smith
PRESIDENT

L.P. Bewell
SUPERINTENDENT

W.E. Terry
SECRETARY

W. H. Welch
PRINCIPAL

METROPOLITAN SUPPLY CO. CEDAR RAPIDS, IOWA

Remember to scan your objects and papers to reduce their bulkiness and more importantly, to insure that the originals can be properly stored and protected from humidity and temperature changes.

Supplies List

Paper: The Paper Company
Vellum: Paper Pizazz by Hot Off The Press
Dye pad: Memories/Sand, Stewart Superior Corporation
Other: Scanned objects
Computer font: Diploma, The Print Shop/Broderbund

The great thing about life is that as long as we live, we have the privilege of growing. — *Joshua Loth Leibman*

A wise man will hear and increase learning, And a man of understanding will attain wise counsel . . . — *Proverbs 1:5*

The last three years of high school I rode to school with Melvin Weise, a good friend. One day Della Theobald rode with us. She was arguing with Melvin and he drove off the road through a fence into Paul Blocks place. He was a good friend too, who I later dated. We got teased often about this.

I played hooky and drove with Melvin and other kids to Vail, Iowa on high school day. Not my idea and we didn't get caught.

I went to proms and graduations and had a lot of fun in class plays. I was also on the honor roll and graduated from Senior High School in Denison, Iowa on May 25, 1934. I was 17 years old.

Senior Activities

Banquet	May 9
Baccalaureate	May 20
Class Play	May 22
Class Day	May 24
Commencement	May 25

This graduation class photo supports Mother's journal entry about her transportation to high school and riding with a certain gentleman friend who can be found bottom row, third from the left.

The black and cream pattern of oval portraits create a motif that was carried across these pages to help unify them.

Magic is present when we dare to dream and step boldly into the light. — *Unknown*

Write on your hearts that every day is the best day of the year. — *Ralph Waldo Emerson*

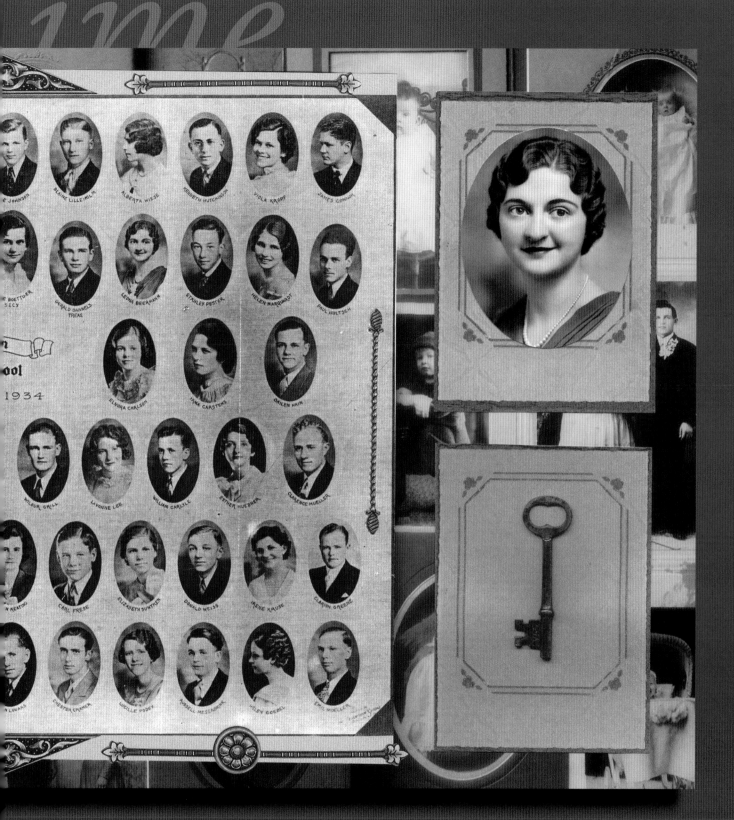

Education is the most powerful weapon which you can use to change the world. — Nelson Mandela

Wise people store up knowledge . . . — Proverbs 10:14

Just as time passes, so do memories pass as well, but those who stirred our spirits sing in our hearts forever. — Unknown

The great thing in the world is not so much where you are but in what direction you are going. — Oliver Wendell Holmes

Supplies List

Paper: Paper Pizazz by Hot Off The Press
Stickers: me and my BIG ideas
Frames: Frame-It /DogByte Development
Computer font: Amaze (Internet)

GOOD OL' DAYS

My mother's (Lena) step-father, William Hoffmeier, her mother, Frieda, and her half brother Walter Hoffmeier.

The "tearing technique" used here gives a viewer the impression of looking through a rough opening in an old building. The layering of different papers adds to the visual depth of the layout. Notice how the intensity of the "milk paint" yellow in the torn paper advances toward the viewer helping to show emphasis as well as create depth.

Photos may remind us of times gone by, but the best ones are not on film,
but deep in our hearts, and in our memories they shall forever abide.
— Unknown

There are two lasting bequests we can give our children;
one is roots, the other is wings. *— Hodding Carter, Jr.*

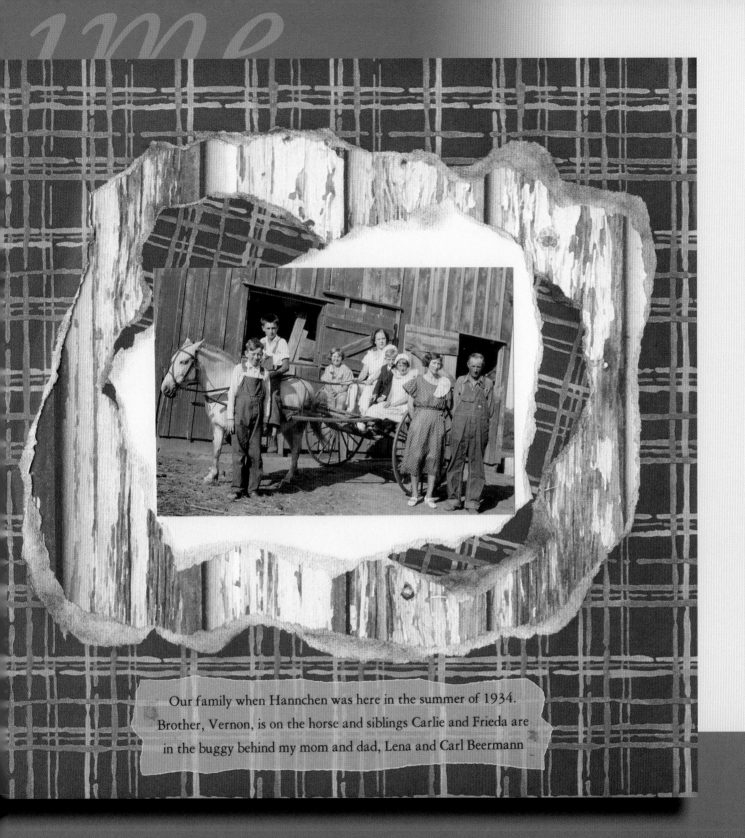

Our family when Hannchen was here in the summer of 1934.
Brother, Vernon, is on the horse and siblings Carlie and Frieda are
in the buggy behind my mom and dad, Lena and Carl Beermann

While the earth remains,
Seedtime and harvest,
And cold and heat,
And winter and summer,
And day and night
Shall not cease. — Genesis 8:22

Lives of all great men remind us we can make our lives sublime,
and, departing, leave behind us Footprints on the sands of time.
— Henry Wadsworth Longfellow

Supplies List

Paper: Provo Craft; Rocky Mountain Scrapbook Company
Cardstock: Bazzill Basics Paper
Vellum: Paper Pizazz by Hot Off The Press
Lettering: QuicKutz
Computer font: Amery, The Print Shop/Broderbund

Strawberry Kate

Strawberry Kate

CAST OF CHARACTERS

KATE WINTON, "Strawberry Kate."
MRS. WINTON, Kate's aunt, living near the town of Cedar Grove.
HAZEL DOWNING, a pretty, eighteen-year-old neighbor.
GWENDOLYN NORTON, a member of Cedar Grove's aristocracy.
MINNIE HOLZAPPEL, a beaming, German woman, who is looking for a second husband.
BETTY CRAWFORD, Bob's impish, sixteen-year-old sister.
CHRYSANTHEMUM KLOTS, Mrs. Winton's lugubrious hired girl.
BOB CRAWFORD, "Babbling Brooks."
CHARLIE GRANGER, his friend.
TOMMY MEADOWS, a pompous and dignified neighbor of seventeen.
EZRA NORTON, the biggest man in Cedar Grove.
JIM TUCKETT, a deputy constable.

SYNOPSIS

ACT I. Room in the home of Mrs. Winton, on the outskirts of the town of Cedar Grove. A Saturday morning in Spring.
ACT II. Same as ACT I. A week later, about five
ACT III. Same. A week later, about seven-fifteen

CHARACTERISTICS AND COSTUMES

MRS. WINTON. A pleasant, friendly, motherly woman of fifty. She is the type that thinks well of everybody. Hair slightly gray. ACTS I and II—Plain, neat, conservative house dresses, which hang almost to the floor. ACT III—Dark, conservative silk dress.

KATE. A beautiful, independent, likeable, small-town miss of eighteen. Small for her age and boyishly slender. Grows strawberries for a living. Strong in her likes and dislikes. ACT I—Ordinary blue shirt, open at neck, and blue overalls. ACT II—Pretty, simple, becoming spring dress. ACT III—A pretty, becoming party frock.

HAZEL DOWNING. A pretty, vivacious, small-town girl of eighteen. Friendly and likeable. ACTS I and II—Simple, pretty, spring dresses. ACT III—Pretty, party frock.

GWENDOLYN NORTON. A handsome, supercilious, small-town society girl of twenty-two. Her father is the richest man in town, and Gwen knows it. ACTS I and II—Modish, costly spring dresses and hats. ACT III—Modish, expensive gown and scarf.

MINNIE HOLZAPPEL. A beaming, German woman of forty. Speaks with a German accent. ACTS I and II—Dark, old-fashioned dresses, which hang almost to the floor. Diminutive German hat. ACT III—Slightly more elaborate dress—her "Sunday" dress. Her dresses are old-fashioned, but not ridiculous.

BETTY CRAWFORD. A friendly, likeable, vivacious, democratic, city-bred miss of sixteen. Always in impish good humor. ACT II—Chic, becoming sports dress. ACT III—Pretty, expensive party frock.

CHRYSANTHEMUM. A slow-moving, rather plain, hired girl of seventeen. Invariably her expression is lugubrious. ACTS I and II—Plain, neat, odd kitchen dresses. ACT III—Odd, gay-colored party dress. Large bouquet pinned at waist. Red ribbon around forehead.

5

Growing up, I remember my mother telling of a play she was in called "Strawberry Kate". Upon reading her journals, it was delightful to discover that she and my Dad were in several plays together before they dated. The cast of characters page reveals the names of those who played each character written in mother's cursive. As you can see, Mom was "Strawberry Kate" and my Dad, Thor, was "Babbling Brooks".

All the world's a stage. And all men and women merely players:
They have their exits and entrances; And one man in his time plays many parts.
— William Shakespeare

As long as we have memories,
yesterday remains.
As long as we have hope,
tomorrow awaits.
As long as we have art,
today is beautiful.

BAKER'S ROYALTY PLAYS
The Cream of Published Plays

Strawberry Kate
by
Eugene G. Hafer

I was a member of our Lutheran Young Peoples Society or Walther League as it was later called. We put on several 3 act plays in the Buck Grove Hall and drew large crowds. The first one was "Always in Trouble" (a comedy), followed by "Parlor Matches", and several more, but the one I remember best was "Strawberry Kate". It was an uproarious comedy. I played the lead part of "Kate". It was in 1935 and Thor started coming to our Walther League. He had a part in the play as Bob Crawford (alias Babbling Brooks) and I was to hit him on the head with a dust pan. The director kept telling me I didn't hit him hard enough. The night of the opening, I hit him harder and he dropped on the floor and surprised all of us. I couldn't keep from laughing, but he got up and the play went on.

When you are lucky enough to have many items with which to develop a theme, you'll want to generate multiple page layouts that harmonize. Mother's theater ephemera pages are tied together by using the same richly colored, tone-on-tone diamond background paper and a subtle leaf theme.

Supplies List

Paper: K & Company
Cardstock: Bazzill Basics Paper
Stickers: me & my BIG ideas;
Ever After Scrapbook Co.; Colorbök
Nailheads: Jest Charming
Punch out: Paper Pizazz by Hot Off The Press
Computer font: Agatha, The Print Shop/Broderbund

Therefore whoever confesses Me before men, him I will also confess before My Father who is in heaven. — Matthew 10:32

CONTINUE ➤

ALL A MISTAKE.

ALL A MISTAKE.

CAST OF CHARACTERS.

CAPT. OBADIAH SKINNER........A Retired Sea Captain
LIEUT. GEORGE RICHMOND........His Nephew
RICHARD HAMILTON.........A Country Gentleman
FERDINAND LIGHTHEAD..........A Neighbor
NELLIE RICHMOND..........George's Wife
NELLIE HUNTINGTON..........A Friend
CORNELIA (NELLIE) SKINNER......Obadiah's Sister
NELLIE MCINTYRE..........A Servant

TIME—The Present.

PLACE—House and Grounds of Capt. Obadiah Skinner,
Otherwise Known as "Oak Farm," Westchester, and
Adjoining the State Insane Asylum.

TIME OF PLAYING—About Two Hours.

NOTICE.—Amateurs are free to produce this play, but the sole
professional rights are reserved by the author, who may be ad-
dressed in care of the Publisher.

MADE IN U. S. A.

Copyright, 1903, by T. S. DENISON
Copyright, 1931, by W. C. PARKER (IN RENEWAL)

ALL A MISTAKE.

COSTUMES.

CAPT.—Canvas hunting coat, corduroy breeches, canvas
leggings, negligée shirt, large handkerchief around his
neck, cap and boots. Same throughout.

GEORGE—Lieutenant's fatigue uniform throughout. Mil-
itary cap in first act, until exit with Nellie Huntington.

RICHARD HAMILTON, Acts I. and II.—Business suit. Act
III.—Trousers torn up the legs, seat gone; coat with one
sleeve gone, the balance in rags; nothing remaining of his
hat but the brim, which is pressed down over his ears; col-
lar nearly torn off; necktie turned around and hanging
down his back.

FERDY, Act I.—Golf suit until first exit, then change to
full evening dress, which is worn through balance of play.

NELL RICH., Act I.—Traveling dress. Acts II and III.
—House gown.

NELL HUNT., Act I.—Morning gown. Acts II and III.
—House gown.

CORNELIA.—Eccentric and old-fashioned garment (a different one may be used in each act.) Always carries a
black workbag suspended from her wrist.

NELL.—Suitable servant's dress throughout.

PROPERTIES.

ACT I.—Traveling bags, umbrellas, hat boxes, etc., for
GEO. and NELL R. Letters for GEO. Wedding ring for
NELL R. Workbag, letters and powder rag for COR. Cane,
letter, wheelbarrow and roses for FERDY.

ACT II.—Letters for COR. and NELL. Gun for CAPT.
Blank cartridges for gun. Burnt cork for NELL. Hot air
radiator, tar bucket, brush and money for GEO. Red fire for
finish.

ACT III.—Towel and knife for CAPT. Revolver for
RICH. Dustpan, wreath of flowers, apron and veil for
NELL H. Letter for GEO.

T. S. DENISON & COMPANY Publishers
623 S. Wabash Ave. CHICAGO

Fold out sheets were needed to encompass the keepsakes from Mother's theater
days. Notice that on all four pages there is only one small photo, which is on the
first page. Don't feel hindered by lack of photos when there is good memorabilia
to be shared.

Today's happy together times are tomorrow's warm with memory times. — Unknown

If one life shines, the life next to it will catch the light. — Unknown

Everything is only for a day. — Marcus Aurelius

St. John's Lutheran Young People

PRESENT

"All a Mistake"

Wednesday, July 10th

Beginning at 8 o'clock P. M.

at the

Buck Grove Hall

CAST:—

Capt. Obadiah Skinner, a retired sea captain .... Emil Niewoehner
Lieut. George Richmond, his nephew .... Melvin Wiese
Richard Hamilton, a country gentleman .... Thorwald Johannsen
Ferdinand Lighthead, a neighbor .... Paul Block
Nellie Richmond, George's wife .... Helen Frey
Nellie Huntington, a friend .... Leona Beermann
Cornelia (Nellie) Skinner, Abadiah's sister .... Rose Lorenzen
Nellie McIntyre, a servant .... Margaret Weller

Time: The present.
Place: House and grounds of Capt. Obadiah Skinner, otherwise known as "Oak Farm", Westchester, and adjoining the State Insane Asylum.

ACT I—Front lawn at "Oak Farm".
ACT II—Drawing room at "Oak Farm".
ACT III—Same as ACT II.

Recall it as often as you wish, a happy memory never wears out.
— *Unknown*

That it will never come again
Is what makes life so sweet.
— *Emily Dickinson*

For all of us, today's experiences are tomorrow's memories.
— *Barbara Johnson*

Therefore, whether you eat or drink, or whatever you do, do all to the glory of God.
— *1 Corinthians 10:31*

Supplies List

Paper: K & Company; Rainboworld Papers Collection by Masterpiece Studios
Cardstock: Bazzill Basics Paper
Stickers: me & my BIG ideas; K & Company
Nailheads: Jest Charming
Other: Scanned play scripts and program

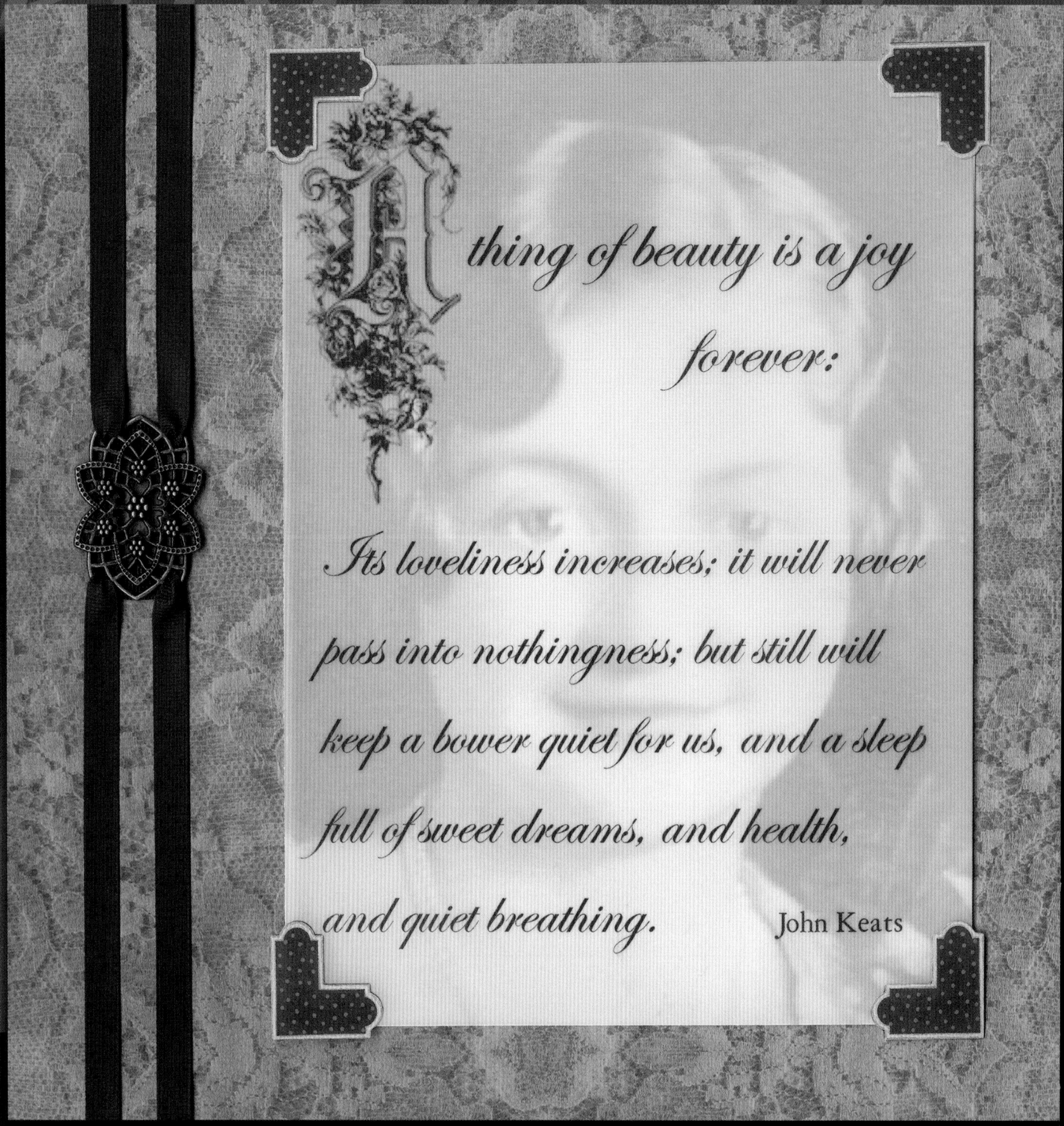

A thing of beauty is a joy

forever:

Its loveliness increases; it will never

pass into nothingness; but still will

keep a bower quiet for us, and a sleep

full of sweet dreams, and health,

and quiet breathing.   John Keats

The biggest and most exciting challenge for this layout was taking the group wedding photo, shown to the right, and removing everyone but my mother, by means of photo editing software. Her face was cropped and enlarged and the tint was reduced to 20%. The edited version was then printed on vellum along with a favorite poem capturing Mother's delicate beauty and dreamy expression.

The metal ribbon embellishments which mimic the lacey background are belt buckles from the sewing center.

Make each day useful and cheerful and prove that you know the worth of time by employing it well.
— Louisa May Alcott

These things I have spoken to you, that My joy may remain in you, and that your joy may be full.
— John 15:11

Love is a great beautifier.
— Unknown

Supplies List

Paper: DieCuts with a View
Vellum: Paper Pizazz by Hot Off The Press
Stickers: me & my BIG ideas
Buckle: Li & Fung, distributed by Jo-Ann Stores, Inc.
Other: Ribbon
Computer fonts: Dover Publications; Amery,
The Print Shop/Broderbund;
Edwardian ITC (Internet)

To create depth in this layout, the edges of the floral images were cut so the photo and journal block could be inserted. This technique can be used to feature charming elements on the background paper rather than overlap and conceal them.

Note how the flowers and stripes in the paper frame guide your eye to Mother's portrait and journaling.

A smile is the light in the window of your face which tells people that your heart is at home. — Unknown

I walk the world in wonder. — Oscar Wilde

I met Thorwald Johannsen in 1934 at a dance at the Buck Grove Hall. I had also seen him in church several times. I was 17 years old and graduated from High School. Thor was 23 years old and had completed one year of college. On our first date we went to the movies and when we got home it began to storm. I started to get out of the car and he said, "I'll take a chance with the storm if you'll take a chance with me". So I stayed in the car with him.

Thor and his family had just moved to the farm from Marshalltown, Iowa when we met. My dad was unhappy with the boys I was dating. He said, "Why can't you go out with one of the Johannsen boys or one of the Arnholtz boys. So the next time I came home I had a date with one of the Johannsen boys and I didn't ask him, he asked me.

He was a very good dancer and we went to a lot of dances, some in the homes of friends. Our favorite music was waltzs' and polkas. We went with Paul and Arlene Block, our friends, to dance at the Columbia Hall. Later we learned to square dance and went with Forest and Mearle Winn and the Smiths almost every night. Marion Lund was our caller.

We went together one year and two months before we got engaged. We announced our engagemnt in September 1935. My parents were happy with my choice. His parents were glad too.

To get the full value of joy, you have to have someone to divide it with.
— Mark Twain

Heaven is under our feet, as well as over our heads.
— Henry David Thoreau

The blue of heaven is larger than the clouds.
— Elizabeth Barrett Browning

Ask, and it will be given to you; seek, and you will find; knock, and it will be opened to you.
For everyone who asks receives, and he who seeks finds, and to him who knocks, it will be opened.
— Matthew 7:7

Supplies List

Paper: K & Company; Rebecca Sower Designs (EK Success)
Cardstock: Bazzill Basics Paper
Vellum: Paper Pizazz by Hot Off The Press
Computer font: CK Signature, "Creative Clips and Fonts" CD, Creating Keepsakes

Wedding of Johanna Assmussen and Adolf Johannsen
September 25, 1907
Johanna born Sept 25, 1882   Adolf born Feb 2, 1882
Johanna died July 27, 1961   Adolf died Sept 9, 1973

Using original photos in your album is not recommended. Working with photocopies allows for more design freedom and protects the original. The photocopies may be cropped, dyed, textured, touched up and/or enlarged. The original photo on the left page was a tiny 3.5" x 5" photo. The photo was enlarged using a scanner and photo software to create more visual impact. Upon enlarging, I discovered a delightful smile (a rarity) on the face of one young girl. Remember this was an era of long exposure times in photography.

Two souls but a single thought, two hearts that beat as one. — Franz Joseph von Munch-Bellinghausen

Standing: *Johanna, Carsten, Rudy and Lena*
Seated: *Dora, mother Anna, Petrea, father Jens and Anna*
1900

The picture on this page was a poor quality copy machine reproduction. Some lines and imperfections were removed but the quality could not be improved any further. Keep in mind that the photo memory is more important than a perfect photo.

Note also, how using canvas-textured matting echoes the canvas of the photo copy.

Supplies List

Paper: Paper Pizazz by Hot Off The Press; SEI
Cardstock: Bazzill Basics Paper
Computer font: Pepita MT (Internet)

A new commandment I give to you, that you love one another;
as I have loved you, that you also love one another.
— John 13:34

1911 Prices

Average Income	$1,213.00
New Car	$ 780.00
New House	$3,395.00
Loaf of Bread	$ .04
Gallon of Gas	$ .10
Gallon of Milk	$ .34
Gold Per Ounce	$ 20.67
Silver Per Ounce	$ .54
Dow Jones Avg.	82

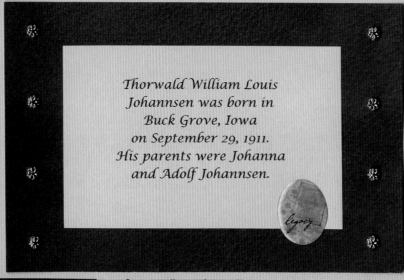

Thorwald William Louis Johannsen was born in Buck Grove, Iowa on September 29, 1911. His parents were Johanna and Adolf Johannsen.

When there is a shortage of pictures for a given event, remember to gather objects, poems or trivia to enhance the page. I purchased a 1911 (the year of my Father's birth) postcard from the Internet.

For this heritage presentation, traditional baby colors were replaced with neutrals creating a more tailored and masculine design.

1911

Thor's Baptismal Gown

The original photo of this baptismal dress was taken in the 1970s and included the orange and green background colors popular in that era. The photo was scanned, the color removed and replaced with a sepia tone, creating an ambience appropriate to the 1911 era.

Supplies List

Paper:	The Family Archives LLC; K & Company
Cardstock:	Bazzill Basics Paper
Stickers:	Karen Foster Design
Poemstone:	Sonnets, Creative Imaginations
Eyelets:	Making Memories
Nailheads:	JewelCraft; Jest Charming
Nameplate:	Nunn Design
Metallic rub-ons:	Craf -T Products
Lettering:	QuicKutz
Other:	Yarn
Computer font:	Lucinda Calligraphy (Internet)

journey

Thor did not want his picture taken so he was crying. Adolf Johannsen, age 31 years and Thor age 2 years.

Thor on his Dad's lap.

Explore

These two layouts were simplified by using pre-designed products that were coordinated with word-tag accents and journal boxes. The result — pages that look like you spent a lot of time, but were rather effortless to do.

What a father says to his children is not heard by the world, but it will be heard by posterity. — *Jean Paul Richter*

Character building begins in our infancy and continues until death.
— *Eleanor Roosevelt*

By this we know that we love the children of God,
when we love God and keep His commandments.
— 1 John 5:2

Blessings abound in a home full of love. — Unknown

Blessed be childhood, which brings down something of heaven
into the midst of our rough earthliness. — Henri Frederic Amiel

Supplies List

Paper: Cloud 9 Design
Journaling boxes: Cloud 9 Design
Green frame: Fiskars Brands, Inc.
Computer font: CK Fraternity, "Creative Clips and fonts" CD/Creating Keepsakes

In the 1920's, Thor's childhood family moved to Marshalltown, Iowa, about 150 miles east of Buck Grove. This family gathering was in front of their house at 605 Bomley Street in Marshalltown, Iowa

Thor's dad, Adolf, and his brother Christopher, owned and operated a tin and metal business called, The Tinshop Marshalltown Sheet Metal Works.

CHILDHO

The scroll motif background paper inspired this layout. The textures and pattern bring energy and a sense of depth to this design. A dry embossing technique added subtle texture to the title block.

The doilies here are actual family heirlooms; their lovely patterns repeat the curvilinear contours of the background.

The scroll-like emblems above the text boxes are "dingbats" and can found in computer font files. These "dingbat" images mimic lines in the doilies, the title box embossing, as well as the scrolls in the background paper.

Parents: Adolf and Johanna Johannsen, both at the age of 38 years. Their children, from left to right are Laurence Arnold Elmer, age 12; Donald LeRoy age 8; Delbert LaVerne age 3; Josina Dorothea age 11; Thorwald William Louis age 9; and Marvin Gerald age 6 who at this age died in a drowning automobile accident.

DD DAYS

The rich black velveteen letters and matting unify and add elegance to the pages. A dye pad was used to color the photo to match the surrounding layout.

Family ties are lasting bonds
That are woven in each heart,
To keep a family close in thought
Together or apart. — *Unknown*

Train up a child in the way he should go, And when he is old
he will not depart from it. — *Proverbs 22:6*

Supplies List

Paper:	Frances Meyer
Cardstock:	Bazzill Basics Paper
Specialty paper:	Paper Adventures
Nailheads:	JewelCraft
Lettering:	QuicKutz
Dye pad:	Memories/Sand, Stewart Superior Corporation
Embossing template:	Chalk Template, FairyTale Creations
Other:	Doilies
Computer font:	Montague, (Internet)

When They Were Young

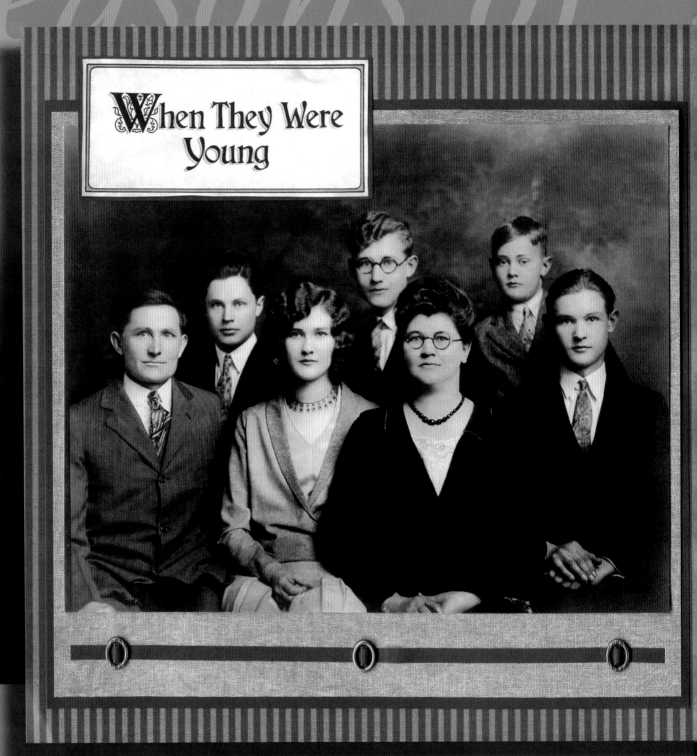

These nearly monochromatic pages have a clean classic, tailored design. Instead of listing names under the group photo, each sibling was cropped from the photocopy and identified individually with a ribbon charm and tag. Paper strips were used in the charms instead of ribbon to coordinate colors.

Don't laugh at a youth for his affection; he is only trying on one face after another to find a face of his own.
— *Logan Pearsall Smith.*

A family is a haven of rest, a sanctuary of peace and most of all a harbor of love.
— *Manny Feldman*

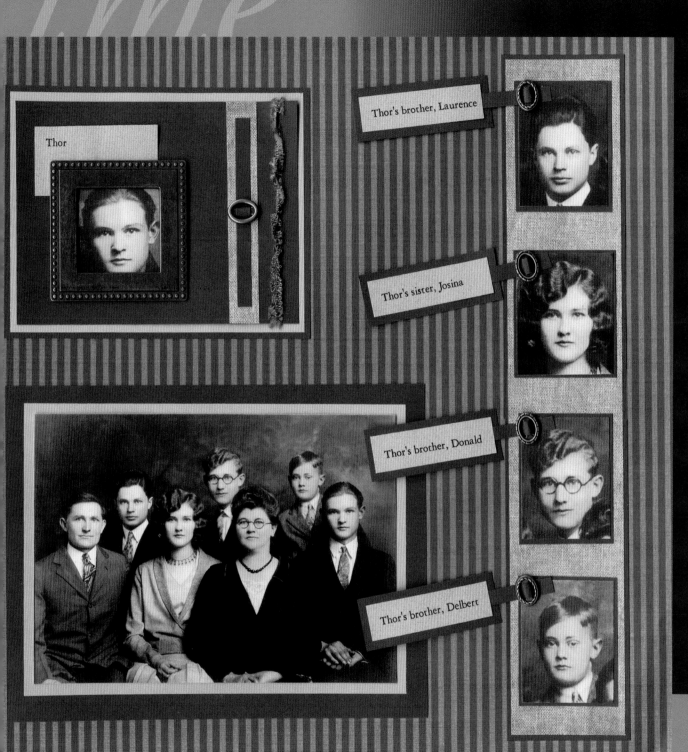

Thor

Thor's brother, Laurence

Thor's sister, Josina

Thor's brother, Donald

Thor's brother, Delbert

Remember now your Creator in the days of your youth . . .
— Ecclesiastes 12:1

Let them do good, that they be rich in good works,
ready to give, willing to share. — 1 Timothy 6:18

A family is the most important unit of all mankind.
It is the core around which great nations are built.
It is the foundation of any great society. — Unknown

A family is a clan held together with the glue of love and the cement of mutual respect. — Unknown

Supplies List

Paper:	K & Company; SEI
Cardstock:	Bazzill Basics Paper
Speckled journaling paper:	Memories Forever/Westrim Crafts
Ribbon charms and metal frame:	Making Memories
Dye pad:	Memories/Sand, Stewart Superior Corporation
Fiber:	Yarn
Page topper:	Deja Views ® by The C-Thru ® Ruler Company
Computer font:	Amery, The Print Shop/Broderbund

Thor's School Days

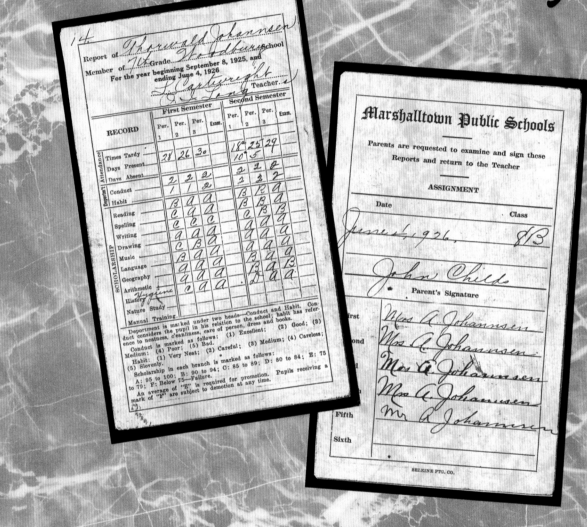

This layout is an example of using only memorabilia to create interest. Once again, scale is important; enlarge the objects to make the layout successful.

Observe how the marble background paper depicts an architectural material that may have been used in a school building in the 1930's.

It is only when we silent the blaring sounds of our daily existence
that we can finally hear the whispers of truth that life reveals to us,
as it stands knocking on the doorsteps of our hearts. — *K.T. Jong*

Man cannot remake himself without suffering, for he is both the marble and the sculptor. — *Dr. Alexis Carrel*

Marshalltown High School

This Certifies That **Thorwald W.L. Johannsen** has completed the Course of Study prescribed for the Marshalltown High School and by intellectual attainments and correct deportment is entitled to this

Diploma

In Witness Whereof, our signatures are hereunto affixed at Marshalltown, Iowa, this _29th_ day of _May_ A.D. 19_31_

Wm. F. Shirley
Superintendent

G. H. Johnson
President

R.R. Miller
Principal

Secretary

There is an eternal landscape, a geography of the soul; we search for its outlines all our lives. — Josephine Hart

The education of a man is never completed until he dies. — Robert E. Lee

The measure of a man is in the lives he's touched. — Ernie Banks.

For we are His workmanship, created in Christ Jesus for good works, which God prepared beforehand that we should walk in them.
— Ephesians 2:10

Supplies List

Paper: The Robin's Nest
Cardstock: Bazzill Basics Paper
Lettering: QuicKutz
Other: Scanned items
Dye pad: Memories/Sand, Stewart Superior Corporation

Thorwald W. L. Johannsen

1931

Marshalltown High School

cordially invites you to attend

The Graduating Exercises
of the
Senior Class

Friday evening, May twenty-ninth

Nineteen hundred and thirty-one

at eight o'clock

Auditorium

Dad's graduation announcement was on a simple piece of white cardstock. A dye pad was used to age the photocopy; then stickers and matting were added for more impact. The photo was left in its original folder for scanning. Many old photo folders have great design characteristics to help inspire a layout and can often be found in antique stores or at estate sales.

A teacher affects eternity; he can never tell where his influence stops. — *Henry Adams*

Great minds have purposes, others have wishes. — *Washington Irving*

THOR

Have regard for good things in the sight of all men.
If it is possible, as much as depends on you,
live peaceably with all men. — Romans 12:17, 18

Man becomes man only by his intelligence,
but he is man only by his heart. — Henri Frederic Amiel

A good teacher is like a candle . . .
it consumes itself to light the way for others. — Unknown

Our duty is to be useful, not according to our desires but according to our powers. — Henri Frederic Amiel

Supplies List

Paper: NRN Designs; The Crafter's Workshop
The Family Archives LLC
Stickers: me & my BIG ideas
Lettering: QuicKutz

Moments in Time

Thor's graduation picture from Marshalltown High School

MHS 1931

The black parallel line borders were remnants from matting another image in the book. Save and file your scraps in clear envelopes to use again. These lines finish the page in a masculine way and develop unity by repeating the angles and colors of the layout.

I augmented this design with a quote, which gives the reader insight into the God-honoring character of my father who is now 93.

We have to live but one day at a time, but we are living for eternity in that one day. — Unknown
The highest reward for a man's toil is not what he gets for it, but what he becomes by it. — Unknown

T H O R

Today I know that memories are the key not to the past, but to the future. I know that the experiences of our lives, when we let God use them, become the mysterious and perfect preparation of the work He will give us to do.
— Corrie Ten Boom

Thor's old shaving brush, pocket watch and knife.

But as it is written: "Eye has not seen, nor ear heard, nor have entered into the heart of man the things which God has prepared for those who love Him."
— *1 Corinthians 2:9*

When I look into the future, it's so bright it burns my eyes.
— *Oprah Winfrey*

Supplies List

Paper:	Karen Foster Design; K & Company
Cardstock:	Bazzill Basics Paper
Stickers:	Nostalgiques™ by Rebecca Sower Designs (EK Success)
Tiles:	Tile's Play™ Sticko® (EK Success)
Frame:	Unknown
Page topper:	Fiskars Brands, Inc.
Dye pad:	Memories/Sand, Stewart Superior Corporation
Computer font:	Amery, The Print Shop/Broderbund

Finally, my brethren, be strong in the Lord and in the power of His might. — *Ephesians 6:10*

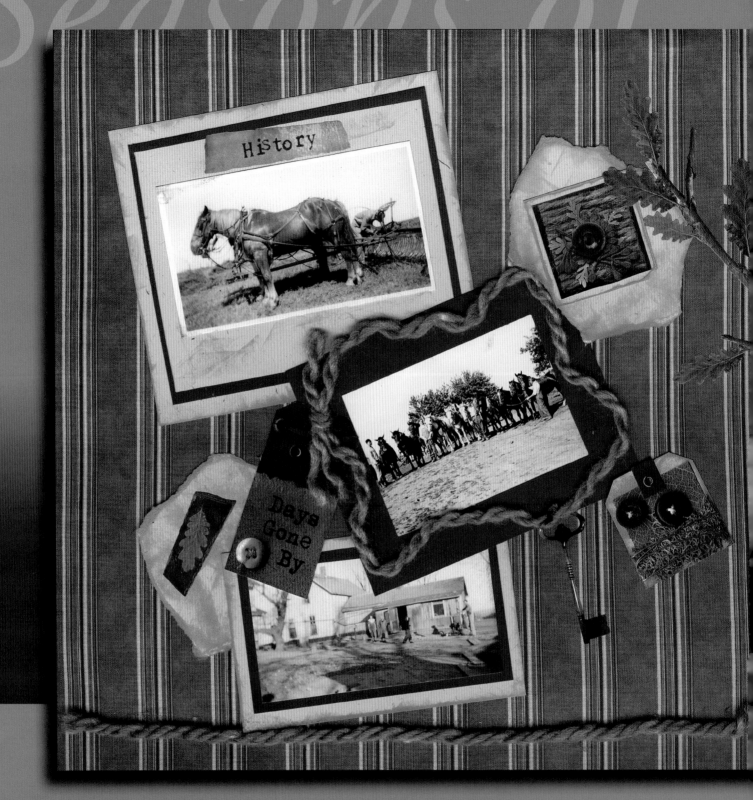

History

Days Gone By

Actual or implied, textures play a major role in the pages emphasizing the farm.

Just as the bottom ties the pages together, the branch sticker flowing from one page to the other creates a sense of unity.

Who plants a seed beneath the sod,
and waits to see, believes in God. — Unknown

He who sows sparingly will also reap sparingly,
and he who sows bountifully will also reap bountifully.
— 2 Corinthians 9:6

Early Farming Days at the Johannsen's.

Their farm was near Buck Grove, Iowa. The brothers, Donald, Thorwald, Lawrence and father, Adolf, are standing with their work horses. Thor is pictured feeding the cows and Adolf feeding the pigs. Farming was a hard way of life for them.

Legacy

I had rather be on my farm than be emperor of the world.
— *George Washington*

This is the day the LORD has made;
we will rejoice and be glad in it. — *Psalm 118:24*

Supplies List

Paper: Daisy D's Paper Company
Stickers: Karen Foster Design
Cutouts: Fresh Cuts ™ Printed accents by Rebecca Sower Designs (EK Success)
Twine: American Hemp
Dye pad: Memories/Sand, Stewart Superior Corp.
Computer font: Bangle (Internet)

Buck Grove, Iowa
August 12, 1934

Hello Honey:

Since you have canned, eaten, & seen so many peaches I called you a Honey which is sweeter than peaches. Since Honey is very scarce and girls as sweet as you are also few & far between the name fit you to a T, but there is another word that beats them all but will save that for later on. Waiting to see what you think about me & how much you care for me. The word dearest make me think that there are many girls with the same name of yours but you are the one that is most dear to me. which you are. But I don't want to put you in rank with them. I put you in a class by yourself. So you can see now that I am peeted.

We haven't had no rain yet since you left. It has sprinkled a little off and on just enough to settle the dust for a little while. It is clouding over again tonight and lighting in the south west. We hope is rain soon for our corn is dry ing up like straw. I notice this after noon that dad I mean your dad's corn field is starting to dry up also. His field north of the pasture.

I sure have my hand full of work now. Dad & Donald went to Marshalltown and also to Clinton they took my Grand mother back home & Clinton she is bothered with hay fever quite bad and we noticed its starting in now. So the work is all left for Delbert my little brother and I.

From
Thorwald Johannsen
Buck Grove
Iowa

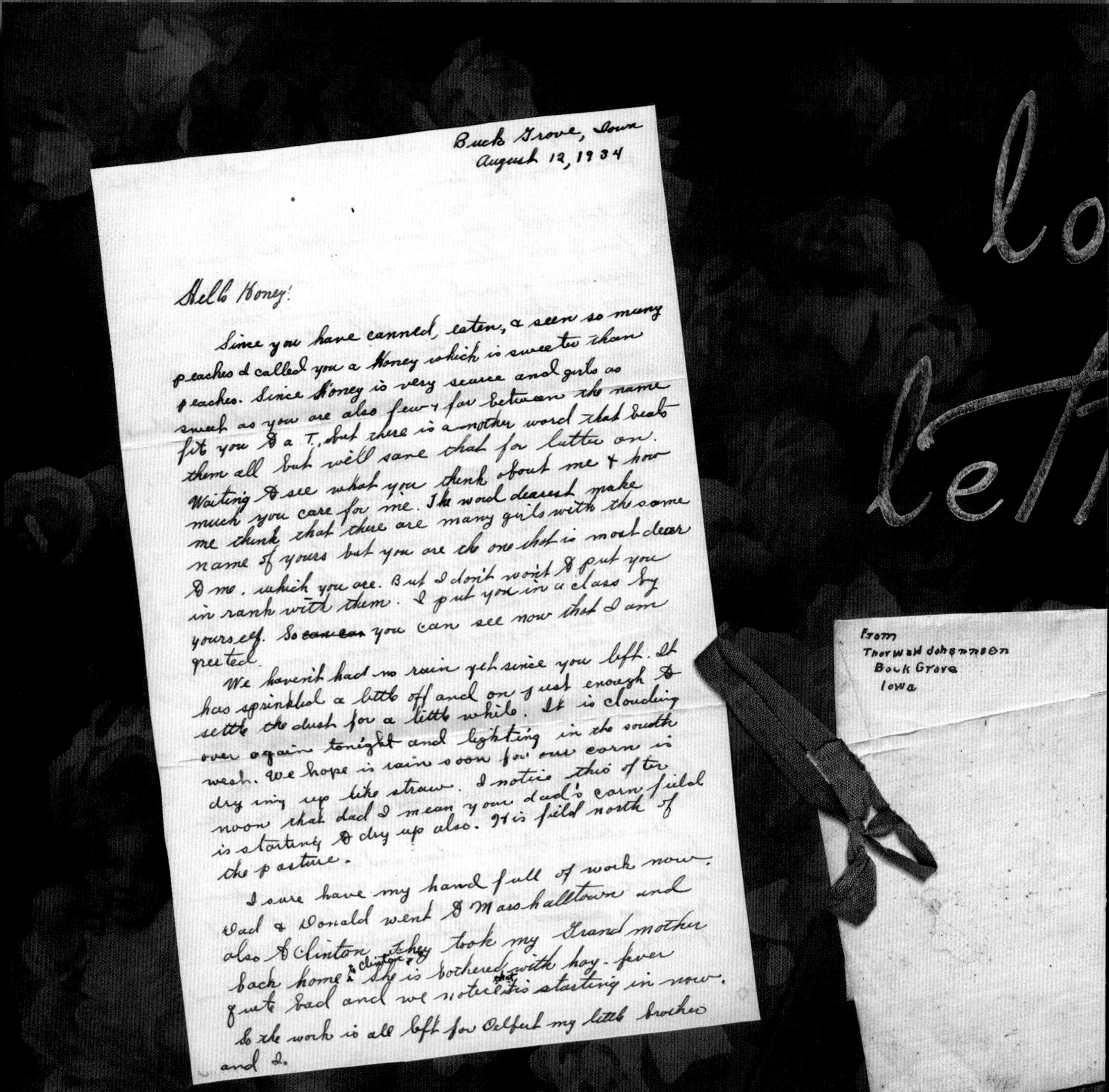

Subtle Victorian floral paper made a lovely background for the gentle romance conveyed on these two pages. The keen observer might notice what a passionate color of ribbon my mother chose to secure Dad's love letters, where he describes her as "sweeter than [the] peaches she's just canned".

Delight yourself also in the LORD, and He shall give you the desires of your heart.
Commit your way to the LORD, trust also in Him, and He shall bring it to pass.
— Psalm 37:4, 5

There is no remedy for love, but to love more. — Henry David Thoreau

It keeps me busy until almost nine o'clock at night getting my chores done.

They had a fire shower on Mr Lee Winn & family this afternoon at their son's home. There sure were a crowd there. I wasn't there so I take my mother words for that. I stayed home and tried to entertain my uncle, who came this morning. He left again this afternoon for Clinton on the train. Our car was gone so I had to ask Lyody Bloem to drive us around.

To-morrow I will have to help bresh Mr Pophen's sweet clover, dig or clean our well out & rake up hay and if that isn't enough for one day's job you can tell me to do some thing else. You don't have to tell me to think about you for a sure is that a plenty. Since one week is past since you wrote your last letter you have only one week left. Is the right or are you going to stay away from me longer than that.

I don't know your cousin but say Hello to her, and tell her to keep an eye on you so the boys up there don't take you away from me. I will thank her in advance so she ought to give me a break by do the above.

It is striking eleven o'clock and it is bed time for a lonesome man so will say good nite which wishing you were here in person so I could say it to you. — I will be waiting for a letter from you.

Your Lonesome Friend
& hus.

BUCKGROVE
AUG
14
A.M.
1934
IOWA

Miss Leona Beerman
Fred Bertram
Ireton Route 2.
Iowa.

And we know that all things work together for good to those who love God,
to those who are the called according to His purpose.
— Romans 8:28

Love is spontaneous and craves expression through joy,
through beauty, through truth, even through tears.
Love lives the moments; it's neither lost in yesterday nor does it
crave for tomorrow. Love is now. — Leo Buscaglia

Supplies List

Paper: The Family Archives LLC
Stickers: Sonnets, Creative Imaginations
Other: Scanned objects

I am so glad that you are here, it helps me to realize how beautiful my world is.
— Johann Wolfgang von Goethe

We were married May 1, 1936 at the Buck Grove St. John's Lutheran Church by Pastor Wm. Frese. Ours was the first public wedding in that church. The attendants were my cousin, Leora Bruns and Thor's brother, Donald. It was at 3 o'clock in the afternoon, on a drizzly day. I wore a blue chiffon dress and Thor wore a dark suit. My colors were blue and white as were our decorations. My friend, Gladys Burmeister, played Lohengrin's Wedding March.

The Ferguson Studio~Denison, Ia.

For added interest or when space is limited, consider wrapping the journaling text around a photo.

To keep layouts fresh use paper design features in unexpected ways. The border on the far right of the next page was the inspiration for a vertical title.

I am going your way, so let us go hand in hand.
You help me and I'll help you.
We shall not be here very long . . .

I THEE WED

The metal dove embellishment was attached using a fine wire, instead of adhesives, to assure permanent placement.

Love does not dominate; it cultivates.
— *Johann Wolfgang Von Goethe*

Therefore a man shall leave his father and mother and be joined to his wife, and they shall become one flesh. — *Genesis 2:24*

Supplies List

Paper: Carolee's Creations
Metal dove: Paper Bliss/Westrim Crafts
Lettering: QuicKutz
Other: Flowers and wire unknown
Computer font: Edwardian Script ITC (Internet)

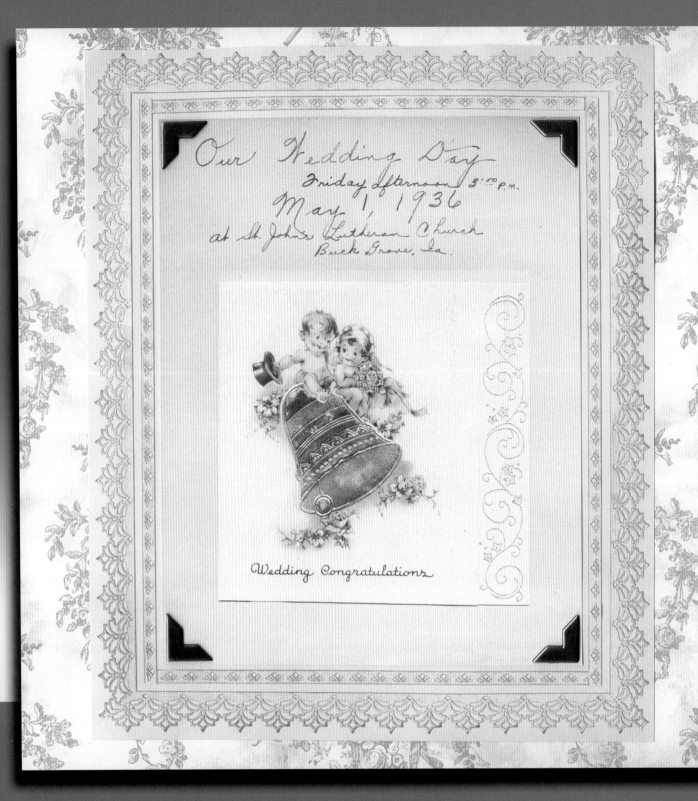

The left page was scanned from a wedding scrapbook Mother had made. The blue and cream background papers reflect the colors in her dress and wedding décor.

A dye pad was used on the lace border stickers to match the background paper of her " Our Wedding Day" page.

Life is a journey, and love is what makes
that journey worthwhile. — Unknown

Faith is our awareness of something greater than ourselves to which we are connected.
— Unknown

Marriage...the beautiful blending of two lives, two loves, two hearts

May they never take each other's love for granted,
  but always experience that breathless wonder that exclaims,
  "Out of all this world, you have chosen me!"
    — Louis H. Evans

Behold, you are fair, my love!
Behold, you are fair! — Song of Solomon 4:1

Now faith is the substance of things hoped for, the evidence of things not seen. — Hebrews 11:1

Supplies List

Paper: Creative Imaginations; Anna Griffin
Stickers: Mrs. Grossman's Paper Company
Metal verse and corners: Making Memories
Other: Flowers, unknown
Dye pad: Memories/Sand, Stewart Superior Corporation

OUR FIR.

OUR LOVE NEST

19

The background paper reminded me of a faded antique wallpaper.
This seemed an appropriate choice for Mom and Dad's 100 year-old "love nest".

The title became more interesting by offsetting die cuts of two different colors.

But from there you will seek the LORD your God,
and you will find Him if you seek Him with all your heart
and with all your soul. — Deuteronomy 4:29

When there is room in the heart there is always room in the house. — Moore

OUR LOVE NEST

When we got home we moved into an old, old farm house (100 years old). We could stand between the dining room and living room and see daylight through the ceiling. It had a built on kitchen, dining area, pantry from which you went to the dirt cellar, living room and 2 bedrooms also a small upstairs over part of the house. No carpeting except a 9 X 12 rug in living room. It was so cold in winter we moved our bed in the living room where there was a potbelly stove. We'd have fire in the stove and tea kettle boiling on top of stove when we went to bed and in the morning, the water in the tea kettle had turned to ice. We moved our kitchen into the dining room and closed off the rest of the house. No bathrooms. Same old "back house" outdoors, as when I was young. Same old black range in kitchen, no refrigerator. This was our "love nest" and we were happy. We were living on Aunt Edna and Uncle Wills farm with Thor's parents, who were renting it. His parents lived in the eleven room new house with 3 bathrooms - one in the basement and running water in house and the works - all but electricity. Still using kerosene lamps though. In the winter, I would go to their house and get water in my pail. (Carried in and carried out all our water). Thor's mother could talk your leg off. One day I went for water and she talked so much and so long, I fainted and fell on her floor. This didn't excite her too much. I was still lying there, when I woke up and she was still talking. We couldn't have company in the winter in our 2 crowded rooms, but in the spring we moved back to the whole house.

36

The beauty of the house is order,
The blessing of the house is contentment,
The glory of the house is hospitality,
The crown of the house is Godliness. — *Unknown*

Even the sparrow has found a home, And the swallow a nest for herself,
Where she may lay her young . . .
— Psalm 84:3

Supplies List

Paper: The Robin's Nest
Cardstock: Bazzill Basics Paper
Stickers: Provo Craft
Lettering: Ellison/Provo Craft
Computer font: Andy (Internet)

With God's Blessings,

This album is to be given to

Grace Adeline Sveum,

my great-neice,
to thank her for bringing joy
back into my life after the
death of my daughter,

Stacey Marie McCloskey.

Diane E. DiSanto

In every photo there is a story yearning to be told. — *Diane E. DiSanto*

Indicate to whom the album should go and include the reason why you made this decision. Notice that the first and last pages of this album are the same, bringing the design full circle.

Supplies List

Paper and Stickers: Frances Meyer
Cardstock: Bazzill Basics Paper
Computer font: Montague (Internet)

*I am the Alpha and the Omega, the Beginning and the End,
the First and the Last.* — *Revelation 22:13*

Internet Web Sites

Excellent sources on how to gather, care for, and display family history are available on the Internet. I highly recommend "Guidelines For Preserving Your Photographic Heritage" by Ralph G. McKnight.
www.geocities.com/Heartland/6662/photopre.htm

Other favorites are:

Genealogy:

www.nara.gov
www.ancestry.com
www.rootsweb.com
www.familysearch.org
www.cyndislist.com
www.genealogy.about.com

Archival Tips:

www.lib.cmich.edu/clarke
www.shopbrodart.com/site_pages/h2guides/text_guides/archival_preservation

Historical Images:

www.memory.loc.gov
www.heritagephotographs.com

Favorite Scrapbook Sites:

www.dmarie.com
www.onescrappysite.com
www.scrapbooking.com
www.scraplink.com/scrapbooking.htm

LOVE OF FAMILY IS AGELESS.

Family traditions make memories for generations to come.

Happiness is an inheritance not to be taken lightly, but to be enjoyed and passed to the next generation.

Yesteryear

OUR ANCESTORS GIVE US OUR HISTORY, BUT THEY DO NOT DICTATE OUR FUTURE.

Dear child be kind and full of love and touch the hearts of all So they may see your loving Lord through eyes so sweet and small.

The smile upon a child's face has worth beyond all measure.

A child's laughter, in all times, remains a Joy.

Childhood memories are never more Precious than when we share them with others.

Silver threads of ages past glisten in our memories.

REMEMBERING OUR PAST BY SHARING FAMILY HISTORY GIVES STRENGTH TO OUR FUTURE GENERATIONS.

Memories are treasures of time we dare not spend.

EACH PERSON'S LIFE HAS MEANING OF ITS OWN, YET YEARNS TO BE REMEMBERED.

Crop – To cut off certain portions of an image. You may crop an image to create emphasis, more interesting shapes, or textures in a layout.

Dingbats – Typographical ornaments or symbols such as arrows, animals, decorative motifs, and bullets found under "fonts" in a computer.

Double-mount – The use of two or more matting surfaces behind a photo or design element.

Dry emboss – To create a raised imprint on paper using a design template and stylus.

Dye pad – A stamping pad which contains a relatively transparent colorant. These pads are found in most craft stores.

Embellishments – Articles such as ribbon, coins, yarn, stickers and die cuts used to make an interesting layout.

Ephemera – Items produced and intended for a short term use which have become collectible such as, calling cards, advertisements, calendars, postcards and invitations.

Font – A group or assortment of letters, numbers, punctuation marks and special characters (dingbats) with a specific typeface, posture, size and weight.

Genealogy – A family lineage or history.

Handmade paper – Paper made of natural fibers found in a variety of thicknesses, density, colors and textures often containing organic matter like flower petals, seeds, or leaves.

Harmony – A pleasing arrangement of elements within a design or layout.

Heritage – An historical account passed from ancestors to their descendants.

Internet – The worldwide networks accessible through a computer and an Internet Service Provider (ISP).

Journaling – The process of recording one's thoughts about living, relationships, and events. Heritage journaling is generally more focused on family life.

Layout – The visual presentation of a page, which requires some planning to achieve an interesting use of balance, emphasis and unity of the elements chosen.

Mat – A paper or cardstock support that creates a border or background around an image.

Memorabilia – Things saved or collected, such as stories, writings or objects about someone or an event.

Monochromatic – A single color scheme of changing values which creates harmony.

Mount – The process of adhering a photo or other articles to another surface.

Muted – Colors and textures made softer, less bold. Muted designs evoke peace and elegance.

Page protectors – Clear, acid-free plastic that protects, covers or holds scrapbook layout pages.

pH factor – A standard measurement of acidity and alkalinity ranging from 1 to 14, with 7 being neutral or acid-free. Acid-free materials resist deterioration over time.

Paper-tearing – The pulling apart of paper to create an interesting irregular edge.

Pattern paper – Paper printed with repeating lines, shapes, colors or forms which add energy to a composition.

Photo corners – Functional or decorative triangles used to mount or embellish photographs.

Stickers – Decorative shapes or designs in various sizes manufactured with self-adhesive.

Theme – An idea, topic, or image used throughout an album to tell a story.

Tint – A color that has been mixed with white.

Unity – The result of bringing the elements of art into an appropriate ratio between harmony and variety to give a sense of oneness.

Vellum – A translucent paper of solid color or printed patterns.

Seasons of Time

INDEX

SOURCE GUIDE

All My Memories
888-553-1998
allmymemories.com

American Hemp
509-466-3640
hemptwine.com

Anna Griffin, Inc.
888-817-8170
annagriffin.com
Wholesale

Artistic Wire Ltd ™
630-530-7567

Autumn Leaves
800-588-6707
autumnleaves.com

Bazzill Basics Paper
480-558-8557
bazzillbasics.com

Broderbund
broderbund.com

Canson, Inc. ®
800-628-9283
canson-us.com

Carolee's Creations ®
435-563-1100
caroleescreations.com

FairyTale Creations
763-424-6627
scrapbookmagic.net

Cloud 9 Design
763-493-0990
cloud9design.biz

Colorbök
800-366-4660
colorbok.com

Craf-T Products
507-236-3996
craftproducts.com

Creative Imaginations
800-942-6487
cigift.com
Wholesale

Creative Memories
888-227-6748
creativememories.com

Daisy D's Paper Co.
888-601-8955
daisydspaper.com

Darice, Inc. ®
800-321-1494
darice.com

DieCuts with a View
801-224-6766
diecutswithaview.com

Design Originals
800-877-7820
d-originals.com

DMD, Inc.
800-805-9890
dmdind.com

Deja Views ® by
The C-Thru ® Ruler Co.
800-243-8419
cthruruler.com

Deluxe Designs, LLC ©
480-497-9005
P.O. Box 8283
Mesa, AZ 85214

doodlebug design, inc. ™
801-966-9952
doodlebugdesigninc.com

Dover Publications
doverpublications.com

EK Success ™, LTD
800-524-1349
eksuccess.com

Ever After Scrapbook Co.
Information unavailable

Fiskars Brands, Inc.
715-842-2091
fiskars.com
Wholesale

Frances Meyer, Inc. ®
800-372-6237
francesmeyer.com

Jesse James and Company
610-435-0201
jessejamesbutton.com

Jest Charming
702-564-5101
jestcharming.com

JewelCraft, LLC
201-223-0804
jewelcraft.biz

K & Company
888-244-2083
kandcompany.com

Karen Foster Design ™
801-451-9779
karenfosterdesign.com
Wholesale